Editor
Erica N. Russikoff, M.A.

Editor in Chief
Karen J. Goldfluss, M.S. Ed.

Creative Director
Sarah M. Fournier

Cover Artist
Barb Lorseyedi

Illustrator
Donna Bizjak

Art Coordinator
Renée Mc Elwee

Imaging
Craig Gunnell

Publisher
Mary D. Smith, M.S. Ed.

Grade 4

TCR 3894

Nonfiction & Fiction
PAIRED TEXTS

NONFICTION

FICTION

- Contains fiction and nonfiction passages on a variety of topics
- Includes critical-thinking questions to improve comprehension
- Extends the reading by using interactive writing activities
- Correlated to the Common Core State Standards

Teacher Created Resources

This is a tapsponder enabled resource!
See inside back cover for details.

Author
Susan Mackey Collins, M. Ed.

D1501103

Teacher Created Resources
12621 Western Avenue
Garden Grove, CA 92841
www.teachercreated.com
ISBN: 978-1-4206-3894-3
©2015 Teacher Created Resources
Reprinted, 2018
Made in U.S.A.

Teacher Created Resources

Table of Contents

Nonfiction & Fiction Paired Texts was written to help students gain important reading skills and practice responding to questions based on the Common Core State Standards. The different units provide practice with a multitude of standards and skills, including but not limited to the following:

- making and understanding connections between content-rich reading materials

- building reading-comprehension skills

- analyzing, comparing, and contrasting fiction and nonfiction texts

- sequencing and summarizing

- experience with text-based, multiple-choice questions

- practice with short-answer responses

- practice in developing written responses to various prompts

- understanding the genres of fiction and nonfiction texts

- quoting from texts to complete assessments

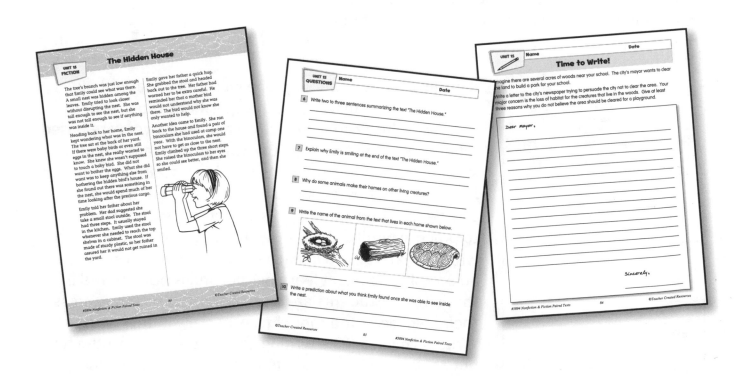

How to Use This Book

Nonfiction & Fiction Paired Texts is divided into twenty-six units. Each unit has five pages. The first two pages are texts that share a common topic or theme. Each unit contains both a fiction and nonfiction selection, as well as three assessment pages.

The book is designed so that each unit can be used separately. The activities can be completed in order, starting with the first unit and working through unit twenty-six, or they can be completed in random order. Anyone using the book may want to look for common themes or ideas that correspond with other units being taught in other subject areas. The units in this book can be used to help teach across the curriculum and to easily tie in reading and writing skills to other areas of study.

Provided with each set of fiction and nonfiction stories are three pages of assessment activities. Two of the three pages are multiple-choice and short-answer questions, which rely heavily on text-based answers. The last page in each unit is a writing page. The teacher may choose to use all three pages after completion of the connected texts, or he or she may choose to only use specific pages for assessment. Pages can be done during regular academic hours or be sent home for extra practice. Students may work on assignments alone or work with partners or in small groups.

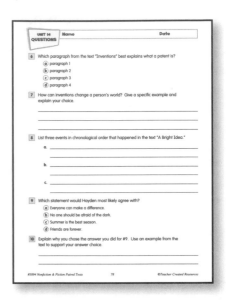

Looking at the answer key, one will notice that not all questions have answers. Many questions require short answers, which can vary, as long as the answers are based on the text. The Common Core State Standards require students to support their answer choices with information from texts, not personal opinions. Completion of the short-answer questions gives students the opportunity to practice writing their answers using information from what they have read in each unit. Of course, creativity is an equally important learning tool and is not ignored in these units. Students are given opportunities to express their own ideas and thoughts, especially in the Time to Write! activities. The writing activities are tied to the texts but are geared to give students the chance to practice the skills needed to be successful writers.

In grading the short-answer questions, teachers must verify that the answers are included in the text. Assessing the responses in the Time to Write! section is up to the teacher's discretion. Each teacher knows the abilities of the individual students in his or her class. Answers provided at one point in the year may be considered satisfactory; however, as the year progresses, the teacher's expectations of the student's writing skills will have greatly increased. A student would eventually be expected to provide better-developed responses and written work with fewer mistakes. A good idea is to keep a folder with samples of the student's work from different times during the academic year. Teachers, parents, and students can easily see progress made with the skills necessary for good writing by comparing samples from earlier in the year to the student's present writing samples.

The units in *Nonfiction & Fiction Paired Texts* can also be used to help students understand the basic principles of text. One way to do this is to teach students to use a specific reading method. Students can use the UNC method (see pages 8–9) to help gain a better understanding of how text is presented on the page and to develop and refine skills for reading for detail. After the UNC method is mastered, students will learn to automatically employ these skills in their everyday reading without having to be coached to complete the process. The skills of good reading will become automatic.

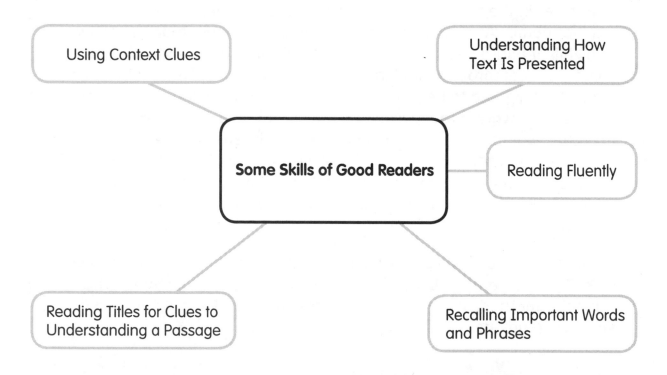

Using Context Clues

Understanding How Text Is Presented

Some Skills of Good Readers

Reading Fluently

Reading Titles for Clues to Understanding a Passage

Recalling Important Words and Phrases

Understanding and Using the UNC Method

U <u>Underline</u> and read all titles.

N Place <u>numbers</u> by all the paragraphs.

C Put <u>circles</u> around or highlight all important words and phrases in the text.

When students are presented with a text, they can use the UNC method to help break down the material. Students immediately underline and read all titles. To better manage the material, students next add a number beside each paragraph. This helps teachers as they go over questions. They can easily ask the students to look at a specific paragraph to point out information that helped to answer a particular question. Using this method, teachers may also discover there are students who have simply not learned how to tell where a paragraph begins or ends. This explains why many times when a teacher asks a student to read a specific paragraph, he or she cannot. The student may honestly be unsure of where to start!

The final step in the UNC method is to circle or highlight important words or phrases in the text. By completing this step, students are required to read for detail. At first, the teacher may find that many students will want to highlight entire paragraphs. Teachers will want to use a sample unit to guide students through the third step. Teachers can make copies of a unit already highlighted to help show students how to complete the third step. Teachers can work through a unit together with the students, or they may even want to use a document camera so the students can easily see the process as they work on a unit together in class. Students will soon discover that there are important details and context clues that can be used to help understand which information is the most important in any given text.

Students need to have confidence in their abilities to succeed at any given task. This is where the UNC method is a bonus in any classroom. When using this method, students can be successful in reading any text and answering the questions that follow.

The UNC method is especially helpful in aiding students to carefully read new or unfamiliar texts. Highlighters are helpful when working with printed texts but are not necessary. (For example, students can use different highlighter colors to complete each step.) Students who consistently use this method will eventually no longer need to physically highlight or circle the text as the necessary skills to great reading become an automatic response with any text. Students who consistently practice the UNC method make mental maps of what they have read and often no longer need to look back at the text when answering the questions! The UNC method allows students who are kinesthetic learners to have a physical activity that can take place during a reading activity. Visual learners are greatly aided by this method, as well. Students are encouraged by their positive progress and look forward to the challenge of reading a new text.

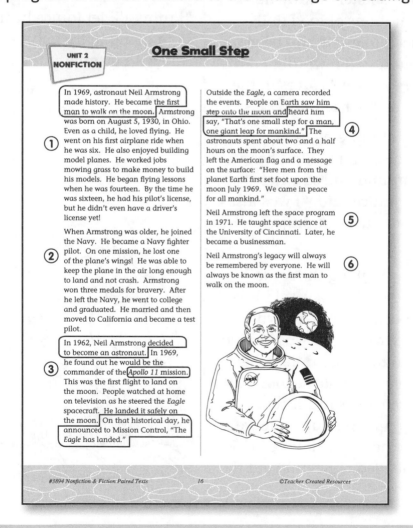

Kara looked at the pages in the yearbook. She liked seeing all the pictures of her friends and remembering what a great year it had been. When she turned to the back, she found the pages that made her smile the most. There were pictures taken of a group of fourth-grade students helping at the animal shelter. Kara knew their class had made a difference. They had spent the day caring for the animals at the shelter. They had helped clean up both inside and outside the shelter. Many had brought in donations of food and other needed supplies. It had been an exhausting but also a rewarding day. The smiles on everyone's faces in the pictures reminded her of that.

"I like looking at those pictures, too," a voice said from behind her. Kara turned around and saw her friend Janice. Janice said, "I was just wondering what our next project would be."

Kara had been thinking the same thing. She already had several ideas. "Since it's almost summer, we will have a lot of extra time. I was hoping we could use some of the time to help out at the daycare here at school. The playground area looks like it could use some cleaning up, and I am sure we could get some new toys donated if we tried. I like the idea of helping out the younger children."

"That sounds perfect," Janice agreed. "I know Mrs. Brown said she would sponsor us, so we already have at least one adult who is willing to help. It feels good to help others."

Mrs. Brown walked over to Kara's desk and stood beside Janice. "I heard you two girls talking. I think you both have some wonderful ideas. You two are great role models for others your age. I wouldn't be surprised to see either one of you become governor of our state one day."

"I think I'll let Janice be the governor. I am going to try for president," Kara said with a smile.

"Well, whatever you two grow up to be, I am proud of you both right now."

Hillary Clinton

Hillary Rodham Clinton was born on October 26, 1947, in Chicago, Illinois. She was the oldest of three children and the only girl. She liked to do many of the things her brothers did. When she was younger, people called her a tomboy.

In high school, Hillary became interested in helping others. One day, a speaker came to Chicago. His name was Martin Luther King, Jr. Hillary got to hear the famous civil rights leader speak. She thought a lot about his words and how he believed everyone should be treated fairly. This also made her realize women were often treated in ways that were not fair. When she was younger, she had thought about being an astronaut. She wrote NASA about her dream. They wrote back and told her girls could not be astronauts. Hillary knew things needed to change. Many people believed she could make a difference. When she graduated high school, her class voted her "Most Likely to Succeed."

Hillary went on to college. When she finished college, she was asked to speak at the graduation ceremony. She spoke about wanting equal rights for everyone. Hillary went to law school. She knew she also wanted to help children with her work as a lawyer.

Hillary would later marry Bill Clinton. Her husband became the governor of Arkansas and later became the president of the United States. Hillary became the country's First Lady. As First Lady, she worked to make healthcare better. She wanted to make healthcare affordable for everyone. Of course, she also worked hard to help find ways to improve conditions for women and children. Another important event for Hillary was becoming a mother. She and her husband had a daughter, Chelsea.

When Hillary's husband was no longer president, she became a senator. It was the first time a president's wife had ever run for public office. In 2007, she decided to run for president, but she did not win the nomination. Later, she became the Secretary of State for her country. Today, Hillary Clinton no longer holds this role, but she continues to believe in her dreams and tries to help others however she can.

The following pages have questions based on the texts from Unit 1. You may look at the stories to help answer any questions. Use the back of the page if you need extra space for writing your answers.

1 Based on the text, which activity would most likely interest Kara and Janice?

   (a) babysitting Janice's younger brother

   (b) volunteering at a children's hospital

   (c) cooking supper for Kara's parents

   (d) making posters for the school pep rally

2 Using evidence from the text, explain your answer choice.

_____

_____

_____

_____

3 How did Hillary Clinton react to the news that girls could not be astronauts?

   (a) She decided she no longer wanted to be an astronaut.

   (b) She decided to go to college to try to become an astronaut for a different country.

   (c) She decided to try to make a change to stop women from being treated unfairly.

   (d) She decided to write a series of letters to NASA protesting their decision.

4 What do the two texts have in common?

   (a) Both are about people who want to help others.

   (b) Both are about girls who want to be married to presidents.

   (c) Both are about spending time with friends.

   (d) Both are about working at an animal shelter.

5 What does the word *donated* mean as it is used in the following sentence?

I am sure we could get some new toys donated if we tried.

   (a) purchased

   (b) given

   (c) removed

   (d) invested

6 Why was hearing Martin Luther King, Jr., speak an important event in Hillary Clinton's life?

(a) She met her future husband at the event.

(b) She made her first trip to Chicago to hear him speak.

(c) She decided to become a politician once she heard his speech.

(d) She was inspired by his ideas.

7 Write two to three sentences explaining how someone your age could help other people.

_____

_____

_____

_____

_____

8 Which is true about Hillary Clinton?

(a) She became the first female president, and she was also a senator.

(b) She became a senator, and she was also married to a president.

(c) She became a lawyer and a school teacher.

(d) She became a mother and the vice president.

9 What will Kara and Janice most likely do over the summer?

(a) They will spend all of their free time swimming.

(b) They will spend part of their free time helping others.

(c) They will have a lemonade stand.

(d) They will each get summer jobs.

10 Which word best describes the people in both texts?

(a) stubborn

(b) lazy

(c) caring

(d) uncertain

Time to Write!

Part 1

Use the space below to brainstorm some ideas or ways you could help improve something at your school or in your community. List four ideas.

1. _____

   _____

2. _____

   _____

3. _____

   _____

4. _____

   _____

Part 2

Read over the ideas you wrote in Part 1. Circle one idea you like the most. Use the space below to write a persuasive paragraph, convincing people to help you make your idea a reality. Use the back of the page if you need more space to write.

_____

_____

_____

_____

_____

_____

_____

_____

_____

_____

Unusual, Spectacular Planets

Manning stood outside on his deck. He looked up at the sky. Since his class had begun the science unit about space, he found himself looking at the sky a lot. He wondered what it must have been like for the astronauts when they first landed on the moon. He wondered whether people would ever fly to space as often as they flew on airplanes. He wondered whether he would ever get to see the moon up close. It was fun to think about, but Manning had other things he needed to do. He had to finish his model of the solar system for class tomorrow.

Manning went back inside. He sat down at the kitchen table. He looked at the sketches he had drawn for his model, but his teacher, Mrs. Malcolm, wanted more than pictures. She wanted a real model of the planets. He had tried several different ideas to bring his pictures to life. None of his ideas had turned out the way he had hoped. "Are you still working on your science project?" Manning's brother Jeffrey asked him as he came into the kitchen.

Manning explained the problem to his brother. Jeffrey was quiet for a minute and then he said, "I think I have the perfect solution!"

Manning worked on his project using Jeffrey's ideas. He worked hard for several hours. Then he called for his brother and asked him to come back into the kitchen. Jeffrey's smile told Manning all he needed to know. "It's awesome!" Jeffrey said.

Jeffrey's idea to use different fruits to represent the planets was absolutely brilliant. He had seen models completed by students from Mrs. Malcolm's other classes, but none had used different fruits. He especially liked the red planet of Mars being modeled by a ripe strawberry.

Jeffrey helped Manning put the project in the refrigerator so it would still be good the next day for school.

"I only see one problem with your project," Jeffrey told Manning. "It's giving me an out-of-this-world appetite!" Both boys laughed as they grabbed some fruit that was not part of the model for their growling stomachs.

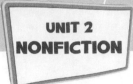
One Small Step

In 1969, astronaut Neil Armstrong made history. He became the first man to walk on the moon. Armstrong was born on August 5, 1930, in Ohio. Even as a child, he loved flying. He went on his first airplane ride when he was six. He also enjoyed building model planes. He worked jobs mowing grass to make money to build his models. He began flying lessons when he was fourteen. By the time he was sixteen, he had his pilot's license, but he didn't even have a driver's license yet!

When Armstrong was older, he joined the Navy. He became a Navy fighter pilot. On one mission, he lost one of the plane's wings! He was able to keep the plane in the air long enough to land and not crash. Armstrong won three medals for bravery. After he left the Navy, he went to college and graduated. He married and then moved to California and became a test pilot.

In 1962, Neil Armstrong decided to become an astronaut. In 1969, he found out he would be the commander of the *Apollo 11* mission. This was the first flight to land on the moon. People watched at home on television as he steered the *Eagle* spacecraft. He landed it safely on the moon. On that historical day, he announced to Mission Control, "The *Eagle* has landed."

Outside the *Eagle*, a camera recorded the events. People on Earth saw him step onto the moon and heard him say, "That's one small step for a man, one giant leap for mankind." The astronauts spent about two and a half hours on the moon's surface. They left the American flag and a message on the surface: "Here men from the planet Earth first set foot upon the moon July 1969. We came in peace for all mankind."

Neil Armstrong left the space program in 1971. He taught space science at the University of Cincinnati. Later, he became a businessman.

Neil Armstrong's legacy will always be remembered by everyone. He will always be known as the first man to walk on the moon.

UNIT 2 QUESTIONS

Name _____ **Date** _____

The following pages have questions based on the texts from Unit 2. You may look at the stories to help answer any questions. Use the back of the page if you need extra space for writing your answers.

1 Which statement from the text is an opinion?

(a) In 1969, astronaut Neil Armstrong made history.

(b) In 1962, Neil Armstrong decided to become an astronaut.

(c) Neil Armstrong left the space program in 1971.

(d) Neil Armstrong's legacy will always be remembered by everyone.

2 Explain why the answer you chose is NOT a fact.

_____

_____

3 What do Manning and Neil Armstrong have in common?

_____

_____

4 Which adjective best describes how Manning feels about his brother's idea for his project?

(a) pleased

(b) astonished

(c) angry

(d) saddened

5 Write three facts about Neil Armstrong before he became an astronaut.

a. _____

_____

b. _____

_____

c. _____

_____

6 What most likely made Jeffrey think about using fruit for Manning's science project?

(a) He went grocery shopping.

(b) He saw fruit in the kitchen.

(c) He saw that Manning had drawn pictures of fruit.

(d) He had used fruit in his own project when Mrs. Malcolm was his science teacher.

7 When Neil Armstrong stepped onto the moon's surface, he said, "That's one small step for a man, one giant leap for mankind." In your own words, explain the meaning of this quote.

_____

_____

_____

_____

8 Which statement best explains how Manning feels about his science project?

(a) He wants to hurry and complete the project.

(b) He wants his brother to complete the project for him.

(c) He wants to do a good job and complete the project.

(d) He does not plan to complete the project.

9 What is Neil Armstrong most remembered for in history?

(a) flying a plane with only one wing

(b) winning three medals for bravery

(c) landing on the moon

(d) being the first man to walk on the moon

10 List in order three events that happened in the story "Unusual, Spectacular Planets."

a. _____

b. _____

c. _____

Time to Write!

Part 1

Imagine you are a newspaper reporter. You have been asked to interview Neil Armstrong after his historic landing on the moon.

Use the space below to think of five questions you would ask the famous astronaut. Make sure none of your questions can be answered with a simple "yes" or "no" answer.

Interview Questions:

1. _____

   _____

2. _____

   _____

3. _____

   _____

4. _____

   _____

5. _____

   _____

Part 2

Pretend you are Neil Armstrong. Choose one interview question, and write a response.

_____

_____

_____

_____

_____

_____

_____

Nora was tired. Camp was fun, but after a week of hiking, canoeing, and swimming, all she wanted to do was take a nap in her bunk. She was glad to have a few minutes of free time.

Opening the door to the cabin, Nora wasn't surprised to find a few of the other girls had the same idea she had. Two of the beds were already occupied. Nora was glad she wasn't the only one who needed a little bit of rest before the next big event. This was the first time she had ever been at camp for an entire week, and everything they did was so much fun. She had so many great stories that she couldn't wait to share with her family.

Nora crawled under the covers and shut her eyes. She could feel herself getting sleepier and sleepier. She put one arm underneath her pillow. Her other arm hung down off the side of her bed. She felt something soft and furry brush her fingers. Her eyes opened wide. She sat straight up in bed and looked down where her hand had been. She was too shocked to scream.

Crawling out from under her bunk and staring straight at her was a creature that was mostly black with a white stripe going from the tip of its nose to the tip of its tail. It was a skunk!

Nora froze. She didn't know what to do. She was scared that if she screamed, the other girls would wake up and start screaming, too. She was certain that with that much commotion, at least one of them would cause the skunk to spray their cabin. She knew she had to make a decision before the skunk decided to do more than just stare.

Very slowly, Nora edged to the end of her bed. The skunk stayed where it was. She managed to ease her way off the bed and across the room to the door. She took a shoe and propped open the door and then waited to see what the skunk would do. It seemed like forever, but it was really only a few minutes. The skunk made its decision. The skunk took advantage of the situation and went out the front door. Nora quickly removed the shoe and shut the door. The other girls slept through the whole thing. Now Nora definitely had the most exciting story of all to share with her family!

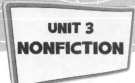

UNIT 3 NONFICTION

The skunk is a beautiful creature with black and white fur. However, most people don't notice the beauty of this animal. If someone sees a skunk, the scent that might be produced by the animal is what captures attention. Skunks are animals that have a secret weapon to use on predators. They have a liquid spray known as musk. Just one squirt of this smelly substance keeps most predators away.

Skunks eat a variety of foods. They can feed on fish, birds, insects, fruits, and other foods. They are also found at many campgrounds because they don't mind eating from people's leftovers or garbage, even if this diet isn't what nature has provided. The most amazing thing about skunks is that, despite their small size, they can scare away predators that are much larger than they are. Wolves and even bears will do whatever it takes to get away from the skunk's horrible-smelling spray. The animals know they need to move quickly to escape the skunk's natural defense. A skunk will rarely miss whatever it wants to hit. It can even shoot its spray from up to fifteen feet away.

Baby skunks are also amazing creatures. Before they can even walk, they can produce the musk smell, which helps protect them. A mother skunk does what she can to protect her offspring. She will stay with her young. She will teach them what they need to know to survive. A baby skunk learns to find food and how to defend itself from its mother. The skunk also learns early that it does not have an endless supply of musk. The skunk learns not to spray a predator unless it becomes absolutely necessary. The skunk tries to warn off another animal first by stomping its front feet, arching its back, hissing, and finally raising its tail. Once the skunk has given its warning, the predator must make a decision to stay or leave. Most predators wisely decide to leave the skunk alone.

UNIT 3 QUESTIONS

Name

Date

The following pages have questions based on the texts from Unit 3. You may look at the stories to help answer any questions. Use the back of the page if you need extra space for writing your answers.

1 What do both texts have in common?

(a) Summer camps are mentioned in both texts.

(b) Skunks are mentioned in both texts.

(c) An animal is sprayed by a skunk in both texts.

(d) A skunk gets trapped in a cabin in both texts.

2 Which event happened first in the text "Hiding Under Someone's Bunk"?

(a) Nora sat up in bed after she had touched the skunk.

(b) Nora came back to the cabin to take a nap.

(c) Nora opened the door for the skunk to leave.

(d) Nora told her parents about the skunk being in her cabin.

3 Based on information from the text, why do most people stay away from skunks?

(a) They are afraid of their sharp teeth.

(b) They do not know a lot about these wild animals.

(c) They cannot see them very well at night.

(d) They are afraid of being sprayed by these animals.

4 Most likely, what would Nora do the next time she went in a cabin to take a nap?

_____

_____

_____

_____

5 Which would be a good alternative title for the text "The Skunk"?

(a) "Nature's Secret Weapon"

(b) "Just Like Cats"

(c) "Camping Buddies"

(d) "Badgers, Ferrets, and Skunks"

6 Why does the skunk warn most predators before using its spray?

    (a) The skunk gets covered in the musk when it uses its spray.

    (b) The skunk has a limited supply of musk that it can use.

    (c) The skunk is too afraid to spray the predator.

    (d) The skunk has to wait one minute before releasing its spray.

7 Think of another animal that lives in the wild.

Write the name of the animal: _____

List two ways the animal is similar to a skunk.

    a. _____

    b. _____

8 List two ways the animal you chose in #7 is different from a skunk.

    a. _____

    b. _____

9 Why doesn't Nora scream when she finds the skunk inside the cabin? Fill in all the answers that are correct.

    (a) Screaming at camp is not allowed.

    (b) She is afraid she will wake the other girls.

    (c) She is afraid that if she screams the skunk will spray her.

    (d) She has a sore throat and cannot scream.

10 What is the name of the skunk's liquid spray?

    (a) poison

    (b) perfume

    (c) cologne

    (d) musk

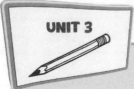
Time to Write!

Part 1

Everyone knows a skunk is known for its horrible smell. Use a thesaurus and find as many synonyms for the word *smelly* as you can. Write the words on the lines below.

_____   _____   _____

_____   _____   _____

_____   _____   _____

_____   _____   _____

Part 2

Circle four of the synonyms you wrote in Part 1. Use these circled words in a paragraph convincing people they should never bother any skunk they see in the wild. Write your paragraph on the lines below. Use the back of the page if you need more space.

_____

_____

_____

_____

_____

_____

_____

_____

_____

_____

_____

_____

_____

Caleb looked at the menu. He wasn't sure what to order. His aunt and uncle had brought him to a new restaurant in town. There was no meat on the menu. Caleb usually ate hamburgers and chicken strips. He wasn't sure what to order. His aunt must have noticed his furrowed brow because she spoke up.

"Caleb, why don't you try the veggie burger? I've had it before, and I promise it's delicious."

Glancing up from the menu, Caleb saw his uncle nod in encouragement. When the waiter came a few minutes later, Caleb ordered the dish his aunt had recommended. He sure hoped it was a good choice. He had skipped breakfast and was very hungry, but he didn't want his aunt and uncle to know that. He just couldn't begin to imagine what a burger made from vegetables was going to taste like. His mother would be surprised by his order if she were here. She could never get Caleb to eat a vegetable. She thought it was funny because Caleb told everyone his favorite vegetable was macaroni and cheese!

Caleb's stomach was growling when the food arrived. He looked at the food on his plate. It looked delicious. It smelled even better. He picked up the burger in both hands. He looked up and saw his aunt and uncle were both watching him closely. *Here goes nothing*, he thought, as he took the first big bite.

Caleb chewed. Then he swallowed. Then he smiled. The food was delicious!

His aunt and uncle looked relieved and began eating their own food. Caleb knew he was going to finish every bite of his burger. If he had known vegetables could taste this fantastic, he would have eaten them long before now. He was quite sure that he would always like macaroni and cheese, but he knew now that if someone asked him what his favorite vegetable was, he might have to tell them it looked a lot like a regular burger! He laughed to himself thinking about how confusing that answer sounded.

Going Meatless

Being a vegetarian or having a vegan diet is one lifestyle many people embrace. However, some people genuinely enjoy the taste of meat. Some people want to enjoy the taste of meat, but they don't want to help the industry that sells meat products or eat foods that come from animals. For these people, there are some alternatives to getting the taste of chicken or the wonderful aroma of a juicy burger. They can choose to eat fake meats.

Fake meats are also known as meat analogs. Meat analogs are foods that look, feel, and taste like real meat from an animal. These foods are made from several different sources. Some are made from soybean products. Others are made of wheat gluten. Still, others come from vegetable food sources, such as beans and mushrooms. The possibilities are endless.

In many countries, people have been eating these meat replacements for years. In other countries, the idea of meat analogs is new. Because the foods are a replacement for meats, some companies form the foods into familiar shapes, such as hamburger and chicken patties. Why take the time to copy the shapes? For many people, enjoying certain foods is all about what they see. In other words, people judge their food by how it looks and not just by how it tastes.

Deciding whether or not to eat meat is a personal decision for most people. People on both sides of the debate feel very strongly about their opinions. Either way, meat analogs offer people another option in their eating choices.

The following pages have questions based on the texts from Unit 4. You may look at the stories to help answer any questions. Use the back of the page if you need extra space for writing your answers.

1 Write three facts from the text "Going Meatless."

a. _____

b. _____

c. _____

2 Write one opinion that you have after reading the text "Going Meatless." Explain why this is an opinion and NOT a fact.

_____

_____

_____

3 What do the two texts have in common?

(a) Both are about foods made without meat.

(b) Both are about people who refuse to eat meat.

(c) Both are about new foods served at restaurants.

(d) Both are about eating foods without sugar.

4 Which adjective would be the opposite of Caleb's experience at the restaurant?

(a) horrible

(b) good

(c) splendid

(d) lazy

5 What does the word *furrowed* mean as it is used in this sentence?

His aunt must have noticed his furrowed brow because she spoke up.

(a) smooth

(b) calm

(c) wavy

(d) wrinkled

6 Which paragraph in "Going Meatless" best explains why many meatless products are made into the shapes of traditional meat foods?

    ⓐ paragraph 1

    ⓑ paragraph 2

    ⓒ paragraph 3

    ⓓ paragraph 4

7 Write the sentence or sentences from the text that helped you to answer #6.

_____

_____

_____

8 How might Caleb react if his aunt and uncle invited him to eat again at the same restaurant?

    ⓐ He would find a reason not to go.

    ⓑ He would go, but he would not order anything except something to drink.

    ⓒ He would suggest they go to a different restaurant.

    ⓓ He would order another veggie burger.

9 Why do Caleb's aunt and uncle feel relieved when they know he likes the food he ordered?

    ⓐ They did not want to have to pay for something he was not going to eat.

    ⓑ They did not want him to have a meal he did not like.

    ⓒ They were best friends with the chef and didn't want to hurt her feelings.

    ⓓ They were worried about Caleb because they knew he was hungry.

10 Why is it funny that Caleb's favorite vegetable is macaroni and cheese?

    ⓐ It is everyone's favorite.

    ⓑ It is not a vegetable.

    ⓒ It is two separate foods.

    ⓓ It is a meat.

Time to Write!

Imagine you have opened a restaurant that serves only vegetarian dishes. Create three new dishes for the menu. On the menu, be sure to do the following:

- Create a clever and unique name for each dish.

- Draw and color a picture of each new dish.

- Write a detailed description of each new meatless dish.

The History of Me

Brent looked at the framed photographs. They sat in perfect rows on his great-grandmother's table. He always liked looking at the pictures. He also liked asking his great-grandmother about the different people in each one. She knew so many stories about them. One of his favorite stories was about the little girl who was wearing the bonnet. Her name was Meredith. She was wearing a bonnet because she had tried to give herself a haircut with a pair of shears. He was told it took weeks for her hair to grow out long enough that she didn't want to cover it up.

The stories with the pictures were great. What Brent really liked the best was just looking at the pictures. He liked seeing if he looked like any of his relatives. His mother said she thought he had his great uncle's smile. His grandmother claimed he had her curly hair. It was fun to look at the pictures and wonder what he had in common with each one.

There was one thing he did not have to wonder about at all. That was who had given him his green eyes. His great-grandmother came into the room, and her eyes lit up when she saw him staring at the photos. Brent's green eyes were the exact same shade as hers. They were the only two people in the family who had green eyes. Brent thought it was special to have something that was so unique.

"Are you ready for another story?" Brent's great-grandmother asked him.

Brent nodded as they went outside and sat down on the large porch swing. He loved spending time with his great-grandmother. He could hardly wait to hear more about his ancestors.

It's All in the Genes

Most young people learn about Gregor Mendel in science class. Mendel lived in the 1800s. He was very interested in the study of genetics. He wanted to understand how traits were passed from one generation to another. Mendel studied more than 30,000 pea plants. He studied the plants to try to understand why some traits are passed on and others are not. He noticed that sometimes a pea plant would be tall. Then its offspring would not be tall. He noticed that the color of the peas could even change from plant to plant. He wanted to understand why this happened. After many careful studies, Mendel was able to gather important information. He understood that some traits are dominant. He could also explain that some traits are recessive and do not show up as often.

Many people don't think about why they are left-handed or right-handed. They don't think about why they can roll their tongue or wiggle their ears. However, a person's genes play a role in creating all the traits that make each person unique. Dominant genes help in developing these special traits. When a gene is dominant, more people will have that trait. This helps explain why more people are right-handed than they are left-handed.

Today, scientists study genetic engineering. With genetic engineering, many individual traits can be changed or made better. Genetically engineered crops are just one example. Scientists can create crops that produce more food and are resistant to different diseases. Changed genes can also be used to help treat certain diseases or illnesses.

Not everyone agrees that making these types of changes should be done, but the benefit of some of these changes can be easily seen and understood by most who are aware of them.

The following pages have questions based on the texts from Unit 5. You may look at the stories to help answer any questions. Use the back of the page if you need extra space for writing your answers.

1 What do Brent and his great-grandmother have in common?

_____

_____

2 What does the word *ancestors* mean as it is used in the following sentence?

He could hardly wait to hear more about his ancestors.

(a) people a person knows

(b) relatives a person is descended from

(c) a person's cousins

(d) someone's children

3 List one thing Brent and Gregor Mendel have in common.

_____

_____

_____

_____

4 Which choice is an example of a genetic trait?

(a) loud sneezes

(b) hair color

(c) sleep patterns

(d) haircuts

5 According to the text, which would be a positive effect of genetic engineering?

(a) People would never argue.

(b) Animals would live forever.

(c) There would be unlimited food supplies.

(d) Crops would be resistant to diseases.

6 Which word best describes the relationship between Brent and his great-grandmother?

    (a) loving

    (b) timid

    (c) angry

    (d) curious

7 Write the sentence from the text that helped you to answer #6.

_____

_____

_____

8 List one reason why genetically engineered genes might be a bad idea.

_____

_____

_____

_____

9 Why does Brent like looking at the pictures of his relatives?

    (a) He likes looking at the unusual outfits the people were wearing.

    (b) He has never seen black and white photographs before.

    (c) He likes seeing if he has any traits in common with the people in the pictures.

    (d) He likes looking for old pictures of his mother and father.

10 If you could pass down one trait about yourself to someone in the future, what would it be? Explain your answer.

_____

_____

_____

_____

Time to Write!

Every person is unique, so use the space below to tell all about an amazing subject: You! Write about all the traits that make you unique. Be sure to include any traits you know you have inherited from other people. Don't forget to describe such things as your eye and hair colors.

Uniquely Me

_____

_____

_____

_____

_____

_____

_____

_____

_____

_____

_____

_____

_____

_____

_____

_____

_____

_____

Rita put her foot in the stirrup. She grabbed the horn of the saddle and pulled herself up onto the back of the horse. Then she adjusted her cowgirl hat a little lower. The sun was bright. The wide brim kept most of the rays from her eyes.

Looking around her aunt and uncle's land, Rita knew she would love to live on a ranch of her own one day. She knew she was lucky to visit them each summer. Her family lived in an apartment in New York City. She loved horses, but she knew she couldn't have one there. For the past three summers, her parents had let her visit the ranch in Wyoming. At the ranch, she could have as much riding time as she wanted.

Whenever Rita got to the ranch, the first thing she did was bring her favorite horse a treat. Star loved carrots, and Rita liked the way it felt to have Star nibble at the palm of her hand. She knew her horse was well-trained, and the ranch was a safe place to ride. She tried to imagine what life must have been like for people who lived in the Wild West. They had horses to ride and lots of wide-open spaces, but she knew they would have spent most of their time worrying about surviving and being safe. She doubted there was a lot of time just to ride or enjoy a beautiful sunrise like she was able to do.

Rita loved riding Star fast. She liked pretending she was herding cattle. Sometimes, she pretended she was a rider for the Pony Express. She imagined trying to get a letter across the country. She imagined how fast she would need to ride to get it where it needed to go. She knew she probably wouldn't have been allowed to do either of those things, though. As a girl, she would have been at home learning how to cook and sew. Maybe she would have been a teacher, but she knew she probably wouldn't have been riding the range. As Rita gently prodded her horse to go faster, she knew she was a very lucky modern girl.

The Wild West

How could you get someone to move somewhere few people live and that might even be dangerous? The United States government knew how. Back in 1862, any citizen who would move West and live on new land for five years could own 160 acres for free. The people who moved had to agree to stay the entire time and to farm the land. Both men and women could go, and many people wanted to try. The people who moved out West became known as homesteaders.

Being a homesteader was not an easy life. The weather could be unpredictable. It was hard on people trying to raise crops or take care of large herds. However, not everyone who moved out West wanted to stay in one place and settle down. Some people moved to the area with no help from the government. Cowhands did not settle in one place. They moved around following the herds of animals as they fed off the open range. (An open range is an area that has no fences.)

Another group of people who moved to the West were those hoping to get rich quickly. People came directly to the area once gold was discovered. Those hoping to find gold flooded different areas of the West. They dreamed of being the ones who would find gold and get rich. Sadly, very few would find a way to get rich quick.

People found it easier and easier to move West as travel became easier. When the Transcontinental Railroad was finished, people could move quickly across the country. The start of small towns around the railroad stations helped create places for settlers to band together. Eventually, the days known as the Wild West ended. People were able to create homes in an area where they no longer had to be persuaded to settle.

UNIT 6 QUESTIONS

Name _____

Date _____

The following pages have questions based on the texts from Unit 6. You may look at the stories to help answer any questions. Use the back of the page if you need extra space for writing your answers.

1 Based on the text, what is one reason many people moved West?

(a) They had relatives who lived there.

(b) They were offered free land.

(c) They wanted to start new businesses.

(d) They knew they would discover gold.

2 What can one infer about the people who moved west looking for a quick way to get rich?

(a) Most found what they were looking for.

(b) Many found what they were looking for.

(c) Few found what they were looking for.

(d) None found what they were looking for.

3 Write the sentence from the text that helped you to answer #2.

_____

_____

_____

_____

4 What do the two texts have in common?

(a) Both mention people searching for gold.

(b) Both mention working as a rider for the Pony Express.

(c) Both mention life in the Wild West.

(d) Both mention people who hoped to see the Pacific Ocean.

5 Write one reason why someone might have wanted to be a homesteader.

_____

_____

_____

6 Which paragraph from the text "Riding the Range" explains what Rita likes to do first when she gets to her aunt and uncle's ranch?

    (a) paragraph 1

    (b) paragraph 2

    (c) paragraph 3

    (d) paragraph 4

7 Why does Rita think she would not have been able to be a Pony Express rider?

    (a) because she is a girl

    (b) because she is not fast enough riding a horse

    (c) because she is too young

    (d) because she is too small

8 Write two words that would best describe life in the Wild West.

    a. _____

    b. _____

9 Using reasons from the text, explain why you wrote what you did for #8.

    a. I chose this word because _____

    _____.

    b. I chose this word because _____

    _____.

10 Why could Rita not have a horse at her house?

_____

_____

_____

Time to Write!

Imagine you are living in 1862. You work for the United States government. You have been asked to make a poster to convince people to move out West and settle.

Use the space below to make your poster. Be sure to include the following:

- Draw and color a picture of the area.

- Write a description of the area. Be sure to use strong adjectives in your description.

- Include at least three reasons why someone should move to the area.

The Coming Storm

Elijah sat on the front porch swing. His grandfather sat in the rocking chair beside him. They had spent the afternoon at Mr. Jones's farm picking corn. They were now shucking the corn and then removing the long, golden silks away from the kernels.

Elijah's grandmother would come out every so often to take the corn inside. It was now ready to be put away for the winter. Elijah knew there was nothing better than creamed corn during the cold winter months. He knew it was hard work, but it was worth it.

A noise from the yard caused Elijah and his grandfather to stop their work. They both looked up to try to figure out where the sound had come from.

A small brown rabbit had hopped into a pile of dead brush, causing a rustling sound to occur. The rabbit froze as if shocked by the noise it had made. Elijah looked over at his grandfather's hunting dog, Larry. Larry's ears twitched ever so slightly. He whined and then let out a bark. He even turned his head and seemed to look straight at the now-terrified rabbit, but he didn't get up. He didn't move. He didn't even try to chase the rabbit.

The rabbit, no longer frozen in place, ran off quickly to hide in the woods that edged the property. Before Elijah could even blink, the brown rabbit was lost from his sight.

"There's a storm coming soon," Elijah's grandfather said.

Elijah was puzzled. How could his grandfather know that?

"Elijah, did you see how much that dog wanted to chase that rabbit? Did you see how he didn't chase it? He stayed right where he was. Dogs don't like to get far away from home when a storm is coming."

Elijah couldn't believe what his grandfather was saying. He had to be wrong. Maybe the dog had just forgotten how to hunt. Elijah watched his grandfather gather his supplies and put everything on the back of a wagon. Then he heard the rumble of thunder. His grandfather had been right after all. Elijah couldn't believe it. They had their very own weather dog!

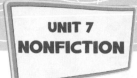

Storms

A daytime sky that turns black is usually a sign that bad weather is on its way. Who hasn't looked up at the sky and wondered how bad the rain was going to be? Most rain is not something to worry about, but when the rain turns into a heavy thunderstorm, it can sometimes be a problem.

During certain times of the year, it is not uncommon to see a storm start suddenly. Spring and summer months are often accompanied by quickly moving storms. Rain is usually not a bad thing unless there is so much that it causes flooding. However, wind from rainstorms can cause damage. Strong winds can take out power lines and even knock down trees. Driving during a thunderstorm is extremely difficult. For those on the road during a storm, this is an especially hazardous place to be. Hail that comes from a storm can also cause damage. Some hail can be as large as softballs! These hard pieces of ice can cause damage to the roofs on houses, to windows, and even to cars. No one wants to be outside when hail begins to fall from the sky.

Lightning can also be a problem during a storm. Thunder is loud, but it cannot hurt anyone; however, lightning can cause damage. Bolts of lightning can strike an object that is outside during a storm. The bolt may strike the tallest object in an area. Usually, this is a tree or a house, but even a person can be in serious danger if outside when lightning strikes.

Tornadoes are one of the most frightening results of storms. Air begins to spin so fast it forms the familiar shape of a funnel. The funnel is a whirlwind of fury that can take out almost anything that stands in its path. Entire towns have been destroyed in just minutes by the violent winds of a tornado.

People should always use common sense when the weather takes a turn for the worse. Stay inside if possible. Be sure to check for warnings given by the local and national weather systems. Above all, stay safe until the storm has passed.

UNIT 7 QUESTIONS

Name

Date

The following pages have questions based on the texts from Unit 7. You may look at the stories to help answer any questions. Use the back of the page if you need extra space for writing your answers.

1 What do the two texts have in common?

    (a) Both are about animal instincts.

    (b) Both are about time spent with families.

    (c) Both are about damage after a tornado.

    (d) Both are about storms.

2 How does Elijah's grandfather know a storm is coming soon?

    (a) The rabbit runs faster than he normally would.

    (b) The silks fall off the corn easily.

    (c) He hears the sound from the thunder.

    (d) He notices the dog does not chase the rabbit.

3 Use information from the text "Storms" to explain why a person would be in trouble if outside during a storm.

_____

_____

_____

_____

4 From the text, what can you infer about Elijah's relationship with his grandparents?

    (a) They work well with each other.

    (b) They do not see each other very often.

    (c) They never disagree with each other.

    (d) There is no relationship between them.

5 Which can cause damage during a storm?

    (a) thunder and lightning

    (b) hail and thunder

    (c) lightning and hail

    (d) wind and sunshine

6 Based on information from the text "Storms," list two things you should do if you know a storm is about to happen.

a. _____

b. _____

7 How do you think Elijah will most likely react the next time his grandfather gives him some advice? Explain your answer.

_____

_____

_____

_____

8 Which statement is an opinion about storms?

(a) During a storm, lightning can be dangerous.

(b) During a storm, everyone is afraid.

(c) During a storm, thunder cannot hurt you.

(d) During a storm, hail can cause damage.

9 Compare and contrast a thunderstorm and a blizzard. List one way they are alike and one way they are different.

Alike: _____

Different: _____

10 Have you ever seen an animal act in an unusual way when the weather outside was stormy? If yes, explain what happened. If no, then in your own words explain why the dog in the story did not chase the rabbit.

_____

_____

_____

_____

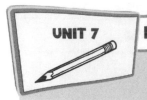

Time to Write!

There is a tall tale that says the character Pecos Bill lassoed a tornado and used it to make the Grand Canyon. Create your own tall tale in the space below. Create a character who captures the wind, the lightning, or the hail from a storm (or maybe even all three) and write a story about what happens after he or she does this.

Remember, a tall tale is not true. The main character is often heroic and can have exaggerated characteristics, such as extreme height, strength, or intelligence.

_____

_____

_____

_____

_____

_____

_____

_____

_____

_____

_____

_____

_____

_____

_____

_____

_____

_____

The Hidden Place

Percy and his friends were meeting after school. They had decided to start a club. However, they couldn't decide where to have the meetings. They all lived in the same subdivision. Being able to meet with each other would not be hard, but deciding on a special place for their meetings would take some time. All of the boys in the club wanted a secret place where their siblings could not bother them.

After school, the boys gathered at Percy's house. Percy's mother had baked the six hungry boys some cookies and had glasses of milk for each of them to drink. They all thanked Mrs. White as they hungrily gulped down their milk and cookies. Mrs. White began putting away the leftover cookies as the boys began their first club meeting.

"The question is where to have our meetings," Percy said.

"What if we meet in my treehouse?" Lane suggested.

Mike spoke up quickly. "You know your sister likes to have her friends meet up there."

All the boys agreed that the treehouse would not be a good idea.

"What about your basement, Tom?" Percy suggested.

"We can't use my basement," Tom said. "My father works nights, and he sleeps there during the day because it is quiet and dark."

"I have an idea," Percy's mom spoke up. "Why don't you boys take some hedge clippers and cut away the kudzu vine out back? There is an old shed that is nearly covered in the vine. You will have to wait for Percy's father to get home from work and get some of your older brothers to come help. That way we know it's safe, but it should be the perfect place to meet."

Everyone agreed it was a great idea. Percy couldn't wait to uncover their new clubhouse.

The Unstoppable Plant

In America, the climate of the southern states is great for growing plants. Plants love the warm weather and the occasional rains that frequent the area. One plant that loves the South is kudzu.

Kudzu is not a native plant to America. The vine was brought in to the United States from Japan. In 1876, the United States celebrated one hundred years as a country. To honor this event, the government held a celebration in Philadelphia. Many other countries chose to celebrate with America and brought gifts to the celebration. People from Japan came to honor America's one-hundred-year celebration as a country. The Japanese brought a vine, kudzu, to America. The vine had beautiful leaves and a sweet-smelling flower. Kudzu would be a perfect addition to America's landscape.

Americans quickly found a use for the new Japanese vine. The plant grew well in the warm climates of the South. People used the vine to create shade in places where there were no large trees. They also used the plant to stop the erosion of soil. The vine was loaded with vitamins and protein. Cattle soon learned to enjoy a delicious diet of kudzu. The plant was quickly dubbed a miracle, and everyone was praising the kudzu vine.

However, the kudzu vine was not the miracle vine everyone thought it would be. There was a problem. Kudzu would not stop growing. Soon, the plant was taking over everything it touched. The vine became like a parasite. It quickly covered the trees it touched. Acres and acres of forest were destroyed by the growth of the plant. The forests that were lost caused a hardship on the other plants and animals that lived there. Their habitat was lost. Kudzu even took over man-made structures, such as houses and electrical wires and telephone lines. Entire buildings disappeared under the growth of the vine. Nothing seemed safe from the invading plant.

Today, people still attempt to use kudzu in a helpful way. They continue to feed it to livestock and try to control the spread of the plant when using the vines to stop erosion. However, those who live where kudzu grows know it is an ongoing process to keep the thriving plant under control.

UNIT 8 QUESTIONS

Name _____ **Date** _____

The following pages have questions based on the texts from Unit 8. You may look at the stories to help answer any questions. Use the back of the page if you need extra space for writing your answers.

1 Which sentence from "The Unstoppable Plant" is an opinion about kudzu?

(a) Kudzu is not a native plant to America.

(b) Kudzu would be a perfect addition to America's landscape.

(c) Kudzu would not stop growing.

(d) Kudzu even took over man-made structures, such as houses and electrical wires and telephone lines.

2 How has the kudzu vine affected Percy's family?

(a) The vine covered up an old shed in the backyard.

(b) The vine was adding shade to the front porch of the house.

(c) The vine was growing along the edge of the driveway.

(d) The vine was stopping the erosion of soil around the family's house.

3 Using information from the text, explain how the Japanese kudzu vine first came to America.

_____

_____

_____

4 Why are Percy and his friends meeting after school?

(a) to try to get a club started

(b) to try to get more members for their club

(c) to try to decide where their club can meet

(d) to try to see if Percy's mom will make them some cookies

5 Using information from the text, explain why the kudzu vine is no longer considered a miracle plant.

_____

_____

_____

6 Why do the boys not want to meet in the treehouse?

(a) The treehouse is not safe.

(b) The treehouse is used by other people.

(c) The treehouse is not close to Percy's house.

(d) The treehouse is too small.

7 Write two words to describe the kudzu vine. Explain why you chose the words.

a. The kudzu vine is _____ because _____

_____.

b. The kudzu vine is also _____ because _____

_____.

8 What does the word *parasite* mean as it is used in the following sentence?

The vine became like a parasite.

(a) something that stays away from everything else

(b) something that lives off other things

(c) something that has a very short life span

(d) something that causes a disease

9 Explain why the kudzu vine grew well in the South.

_____

_____

_____

10 What do you think would be the best way to control the kudzu vine's growth? Explain your answer.

_____

_____

_____

Time to Write!

Imagine the beautiful kudzu vine has taken over your homework. On the leaves, write five different reasons why you need the vine to give you back your homework.

Something Extra: On the back of the page, come up with five different reasons why the kudzu vine should keep your homework.

The Great Ride

Saylor Thomas looked out the window of the train. Her mother and father sat beside her. Her brother and sister were on the seat across from her. Saylor could tell by the looks on their faces that they were just as excited as she was. They were all about to take their first train ride.

The Thomas family was on vacation. They were at an amusement park in East Tennessee. The park had a working, coal-fired steam engine train. The train would take them on a short ride through the mountains. Saylor knew the ride was only a few miles, but she still could not wait for it to start. Her class in school had studied the history of railroads across America. She had read all about the building of the Transcontinental Railroad. Whenever the teacher had read the passages from the textbook, Saylor had tried to imagine what traveling by train would be like. Now, she was finally going to find out.

"Have you ever ridden a train?" Saylor asked her parents.

"Yes," her father said, "but it was many years ago. Your mother and I boarded a train in Kentucky. It was not like this train, though. We spent the night on the train and slept in small compartments with bunk beds. We also dined on board the train. If you all enjoy this ride, maybe we can take our vacation next year on an extended train ride."

Everyone looked pleased with the idea. Before Saylor could say anything back, the whistle of the train began to blow. Saylor felt the train begin to move underneath her. The slow and steady rhythm of the train began to carry them away from the train station and down the tracks. The train's movement caused a wonderful breeze to blow across their faces.

The train ride was everything Saylor had imagined it would be. She could not wait to ride a train again!

In the early 1800s, trains began to become an important part of transportation in the United States. Steam-powered locomotives could haul trains across the iron rails. Trains offered a new way to move both goods and people.

The designs of trains changed over the years. With each improvement, trains became safer and faster. What people wanted most was a train that could travel across the country. To make this possible, miles and miles of tracks had to be added. The idea of a transcontinental railroad in America would eventually happen. The railroad would go from one coast to the other coast.

Construction of the Transcontinental Railroad began in 1863 during the Civil War. Much work had to be done to make the land ready for the tracks. Huge amounts of rock had to be removed from mountains. Bridges had to be built over bodies of water. Thousands of workers had to be hired to help make the project happen. The railroad was finally completed in 1869.

Despite the new Transcontinental Railroad, there were still many problems that needed to be solved for train travel to be quick and safe. Systems had to be developed to keep trains from using the same track at the same time. Bridges had to be kept safe to stop trains from collapsing into the water below. People in charge of the daily schedules had to come up with a system to help people know how long their trips by train would take. They had to know when each train would arrive at its station. Different railroad companies had to learn to work together for train travel to become safe for the passengers and their cargo.

Although many people travel by automobiles and planes now, riding the rails will always be a part of America's history and its future.

The following pages have questions based on the texts from Unit 9. You may look at the stories to help answer any questions. Use the back of the page if you need extra space for writing your answers.

1 Write two to three sentences to summarize the text "The Great Ride."

_____

_____

_____

_____

_____

2 What do the two texts have in common?

ⓐ Both are about the future.

ⓑ Both are about amusement parks.

ⓒ Both are about vacations.

ⓓ Both are about trains.

3 How will Saylor most likely react if she gets a chance to ride another train?

ⓐ She will not want to ride a different train.

ⓑ She will want to ride the train.

ⓒ She will only ride if her brother and sister can ride, too.

ⓓ She will never ride another train.

4 Why are trains not as popular today as they were in the past?

ⓐ People do not like the noise of the trains.

ⓑ People have other ways to travel, such as automobiles and airplanes.

ⓒ People cannot afford the price of the tickets.

ⓓ People are afraid of traveling by train.

5 Write one fact from the text "Transportation on the Tracks."

_____

_____

_____

6 List three events in chronological order from the text "The Great Ride."

First, _____

_____

Next, _____

_____

Finally, _____

_____

7 Which paragraph in the nonfiction text best explains the obstacles that made it hard to build the Transcontinental Railroad?

    (a) paragraph 1

    (b) paragraph 2

    (c) paragraph 3

    (d) paragraph 4

8 Which word best describes Saylor's personality?

    (a) shy

    (b) adventurous

    (c) friendly

    (d) sweet

9 Which major war was being fought during the construction of the transcontinental railroad?

    (a) the Civil War

    (b) the Revolutionary War

    (c) World War I

    (d) World War II

10 What does the word *goods* mean as it is used in the following sentence?

Trains offered a new way to move both goods and people.

_____

_____

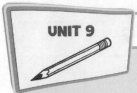
Time to Write!

Trains can take people to faraway places. Choose somewhere you would like to travel. With your teacher's help, do some research about your special place. Then answer the questions below.

Where would you like to travel? _____

Can you get there by train? _____

How would you choose to get there? _____

What would you want to do or see while you were there? _____

_____

_____

_____

Why did you choose this place? _____

_____

_____

_____

Who would travel with you? _____

_____

_____

_____

What is one thing you would not leave home without taking? Why? _____

_____

_____

_____

Something Extra: On the back of the page, draw and color a picture of you at your special place.

All of the students from Mrs. Mallory's class walked quietly into the library. Jack was curious about what the day would be like. He knew today was a special day. The fourth graders were not there to check out books. They were meeting in the library for a presentation. A group from a wildlife rehabilitation shelter was visiting the school. The people at the shelter help animals from the wild that are hurt. Jack's teacher had told everyone in the class that some of the animals would be able to go back into the wild. Other animals would have to always live at the shelter. Mrs. Mallory had told the students they would get to see some of the animals, but they would not be able to touch any of them.

As the students took their seats, they saw four cages. The cages were covered with cloths. Jack thought he saw brown feathers peeking out from one of the cages. The class listened as a woman from the shelter talked about the animals.

Jack listened carefully as she told the students what they would see. Two animals were reptiles. One animal was a mammal. The final animal was a bird. Over the next thirty minutes, the class got to see a snake, a turtle, and an opossum. Jack sat up a little straighter as she brought out the final animal. It was an owl! The bird was no bigger than Jack's two hands. Jack listened as she explained what had happened to the owl. He was blind in one eye after he had been hit by a car. The owl had been trying to get food out of a paper bag that had been thrown out on the side of the road. The bag had food inside. A mouse had gone in after the food. The owl had seen the bag move and went after it. At the same time, a car came by and hit the owl. Sadly, the owl would never be able to go back into the wild and survive. The people at the shelter, however, would love and take care of the amazing bird.

Before Jack went back to class, he asked his teacher if he could ask one last question. He wanted to know if the shelter had volunteers who worked there. Jack was glad to hear that her answer was yes.

Amazing Owls

Owls can be found on almost every continent in the world, except Antarctica. Because owls live in different places, there are various types of owls. Owls come in many different colors. Their feathers are usually colored to blend in with particular habitats. This helps keep them safe from predators and helps them hunt.

Most owls have some features that are similar. They usually have round faces and big eyes. Their sharp bill is also a feature that makes them stand out from other animals. Their ear tufts are another special feature. The feathers that stick up on the heads of many owls are not ears but tufts. An owl's ears are on the side of its head just like yours! Another special thing about most owls is the amount of feathers that cover their bodies. Many owls have feathers that cover their legs and their feet.

Owls are nocturnal creatures. Their bodies were made to search for prey in the evening light. They have excellent senses that help them find their prey in the dark. Owls have large eyes that help them see well, but they cannot move their eyes like a person can. Instead, an owl moves its head to see all around. In fact, an owl can move its head so far around that it can see what is behind it! Not only do owls have amazing sight, but they also have incredible hearing. They can hear an animal as small as a mouse over great distances. These features, along with their incredible ability to fly and their sharp claws and beaks, make the owl the ultimate night predator.

Once an owl has captured its prey, it is time for it to eat. Owls are very neat eaters because they eat everything! They swallow their prey whole. This means they eat even the bones and fur of whatever they catch. The owl cannot digest all of what it swallows, so things can get a little messy. The things that cannot be digested become small pellets, and the owl spits them back out! Anyone brave enough to dig through an owl pellet can usually tell what the owl ate for dinner.

The following pages have questions based on the texts from Unit 10. You may look at the stories to help answer any questions. Use the back of the page if you need extra space for writing your answers.

1 Why did the students most likely need to be quiet when they walked into the library?

   (a) because people were reading

   (b) because people were studying

   (c) because people's voices could scare the animals

   (d) because the teacher had a headache

2 Which paragraph in the text "Wildlife Adventure" best explains why the students were visiting the library?

   (a) paragraph 1

   (b) paragraph 2

   (c) paragraph 3

   (d) paragraph 4

3 Why did Jack ask one last question?

   (a) He wanted to know about volunteering at the shelter.

   (b) He did not want to go back to class.

   (c) He wanted to find out more about owls.

   (d) He knew the lady from the shelter.

4 One of the texts is titled "Amazing Owls." Using this text, list two reasons why owls are amazing creatures.

   a. _____

   b. _____

5 Why do owls have different colored feathers? Fill in **all** the answers that are correct.

   (a) to help them blend in with their habitats

   (b) to help them be better predators

   (c) to help them hide from their prey

   (d) to help them fly better

6   Explain the purpose of the wildlife shelter.

_____

_____

_____

_____

7   If Jack has the opportunity to volunteer at the shelter, what will he most likely do?

   (a) turn down the opportunity

   (b) decide to help

   (c) help if some of his friends will also go to help

   (d) give the shelter some money but not any of his time

8   What do the two texts have in common?

_____

_____

_____

9   Write an opinion someone might have about owls.

_____

_____

_____

_____

10   Why could the owl from the shelter not be returned to the wild?

   (a) The owl could no longer fly.

   (b) The owl was blind in one eye.

   (c) The owl had lost one of its legs.

   (d) The owl was scared of loud noises.

Time to Write!

People usually say certain animals make certain sounds. A dog goes "woof," or a cat goes "meow." Most people say an owl goes "hoo" or "who." Try thinking like an owl sounds and answer the "who" questions below.

1. Who is someone you have known for a long time?

   _____

2. Who is someone from history you would like to learn more about?

   _____

3. Who is your favorite actor or singer?

   _____

4. Who are some people in your family?

   _____

5. Who is your teacher?

   _____

6. Who do you think has an amazing smile?

   _____

7. Who is someone you would do something nice for?

   _____

8. Who is someone who has done something nice for you?

   _____

9. Who is someone you hope you will always know?

   _____

10. Who is someone you have always dreamed of meeting?

   _____

Something Extra: On the back of the page, write a short paragraph explaining who you most admire and why.

Malcolm loved being at the beach. His family came every spring when school was closed for break. They had been coming to the same beach for as long as he could remember. They stayed in a house they rented that was built across from the ocean. It had tall stilts underneath it to keep it safe from rising water.

Malcolm's mother always brought a picnic lunch when they went out for the day. She set up the beach umbrella so they would have shade while they ate. She used the top of the cooler like a small table. Everyone spread out beach towels and sat underneath the shade to eat lunch.

When Malcolm saw everyone gathering under the umbrella, he knew it was time to eat. He quickly left the water to join the others. He was hungry from a morning of swimming and playing. Everyone enjoyed the picnic outside, and then they all rested on their beach towels before heading back out to swim.

Jonathan, Malcolm's older brother, loved using their small boards and riding the waves with Malcolm. They would go out into the ocean and wait for a wave to start. Then they would lie across the boards and ride them into the shore. The two brothers saw a large wave coming. They quickly got on their boards and anxiously awaited their fun ride. Jonathan took off just fine, but Malcolm did not get on his board in time. The giant wave pushed him down. He came up with a mouthful of ocean water.

Jonathan rushed out to Malcolm to make sure he was okay. "Are you all right, little brother?"

Malcolm grinned. "I'm fine. I just got a mouthful of salt water."

"Well, that's not too bad," Jonathan said. "You did just have lunch. A little salt with your food is always a tasty treat!" Then Jonathan quickly swam back out into the water before his brother decided to help him get his own salty snack.

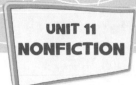

Salt of the Earth

Have you ever heard someone say, "He's the salt of the earth," or "He's worth his salt"? There is a reason why something as simple as salt shows up in some of our old expressions. Today, salt is inexpensive and easy for people to have. However, long ago, this was not the case. In some cases, salt used to be worth as much as gold! Roman soldiers used to get part of their pay in salt. In fact, the word *salary*, which is how much someone gets paid, comes from the Latin word *salarium*, which means salt. That shows how important salt was to the ancient world.

Today, people mainly think about salt as a spice to add to their food. We find it at restaurants and sitting in shakers on the table. We usually think about salt and pepper as though they are a set of spices that must be used together.

In ancient times, this spice was important to people's survival. Salt was the main way people preserved their foods. Then, people did not know how to can foods, and of course there were no refrigerators or freezers. Salt was important to keep foods from spoiling. Of course, salt is important for more than just this. A person's body actually needs some salt to thrive. Just as a person's cells need water, those cells also need some salt to be healthy.

Long ago, salt was hard to get. People could not simply go to the grocery store and buy a container of salt. People long ago got salt from the ocean. Trying to get the salt took them a long time, and it was hard work to separate the salt from the other elements. Salt could also be mined. This means it could be found in the earth. People began to have salt mines. However, this, too, took much effort and a lot of time.

Today, people no longer need salt to keep foods from spoiling. There are many alternatives to using salt. The price of salt may no longer be equal to gold, but there are many people who still enjoy this precious seasoning. Think about that the next time you hear someone say, "Please pass the salt."

The following pages have questions based on the texts from Unit 11. You may look at the stories to help answer any questions. Use the back of the page if you need extra space for writing your answers.

1 Why is Malcolm's family's beach house built on stilts?

    (a) to give the family a better view

    (b) to give the family a place underneath the house to park their car

    (c) to keep the house safe from rising waters

    (d) to keep the house out of the sand

2 List three events in chronological order from the text "Sand and Salt."

    a. _____

    _____

    b. _____

    _____

    c. _____

    _____

3 According to the text, which is a true statement about salt?

    (a) Salt was used to preserve foods.

    (b) Salt is still an expensive spice.

    (c) Salt was used to build houses in the ancient world.

    (d) Salt was never important to people who lived long ago.

4 Which would be a good alternative title for the text "Salt of the Earth"?

    (a) "Salt as a Spice"

    (b) "Salt and Pepper"

    (c) "Salt's Ancient Past"

    (d) "Salt, Sand, and Sea"

5 Define the Latin word *salarium*.

_____

6 What is one reason why salt was worth so much in ancient times?

  (a) It was hard to get.

  (b) It tasted so delicious.

  (c) It was solid white.

  (d) It was extremely sweet.

7 What happened to Malcolm when the wave pushed him down into the water?

_____

_____

8 What do the two texts mainly have in common?

  (a) water

  (b) sun

  (c) salt

  (d) sand

9 What does the word *preserved* mean as it is used in the following sentence?

Salt was the main way people preserved their foods.

  (a) threw away

  (b) kept fresh

  (c) hid away

  (d) left alone

10 Give an example of something else from the past that was once very important but is not as valuable today. Explain your answer.

_____

_____

_____

_____

Time to Write!

If someone is described as "the salt of the earth," it means they are one of the best. Think of someone you know who could be described as "the salt of the earth." Write about the person, and be sure to include at least three reasons why this person is one of the best people you know.

The person I am writing about is _____.

This person is "the salt of the earth" because _____

_____

_____

_____

_____

_____

_____.

This person is also special because _____

_____

_____

_____

_____

_____

_____.

Something Extra: You are a very special person! Use the back of the page to write about the reasons why you are "the salt of the earth."

Digging for Fossils

Elsa dug her fingers through the sand. She loved the feel of the warm grains as they slipped through her fingers. But what she loved even more was what she might find underneath all the sand.

Each year, her parents had a carnival at their house. The carnival was to raise money for a local charity. They invited children from Elsa's school to attend the event. Everyone loved coming because there were always so many fun activities. Everyone also liked knowing the money they spent was going to help other people.

Some of the events each year were new. Some of the events stayed the same. The fossil dig was one event that was at the carnival every year. Elsa was in charge of the site. Her parents built a large box. They filled it with sand. Then they ordered items to hide in the sand. Children would be allowed to use special tools to dig around in the sand and make their discoveries. Everyone liked looking through the sand.

Elsa put on her hat and got ready for her first round of visitors. It was time for the carnival to begin. She used a small shovel and stirred the sand one last time to make sure the fossils would be a little harder to find. She also made sure there were several sieves the visitors could use to help sift through the sand.

Working the carnival each year gave Elsa a wonderful feeling. She liked helping others. She also knew what she wanted to do when she grew up. She wanted to be a paleontologist. She would be able to study things that had lived in the past. Maybe she would find a new dinosaur. Right now, however, she had to focus on the present. Maybe some of the children who came to her today would want to grow up to become paleontologists, too!

Job in the Dirt

Some people have jobs in which they study things from the past. One of these jobs is a paleontologist. Paleontologists study things that died long before people kept written records. They study the fossils of things from long ago. The information they learn from the fossils helps us know what life was like in the past. So what is a fossil? A fossil is a remain from a plant or animal that is preserved. Paleontologists can also study clues left from animals, such as animal tracks.

A paleontologist spends his or her time studying prehistoric remains. Prehistoric means before history was recorded. These special scientists work in an area called an excavation. The excavation is the digging site where fossils have been found.

Paleontologists use special tools to do their work. Because fossils are fragile, paleontologists must be very careful when they dig. Some fossils are brushed with glue to help stop them from being damaged. Fossils are usually not studied at the original site. They are carefully packed up and sent back to a place where scientists can closely study them. Once the fossils arrive, scientists begin using other tools to extract or take out any bits of dirt or rock that remain on the fossil.

The part of the paleontologist's job that most people get to see is after a fossil is put on display. Most people like seeing the bones of a dinosaur after they are put together and then put on display. Of course, the scientists are always learning about the remains they find. When they find the bones of a dinosaur, they don't always know if they are reconstructing the ancient animal correctly. Sometimes, other new discoveries help them know if they have the makeup of the fossil correct.

Studying the past is an important job. The scientists who study the world's past help us understand what things were like years ago. In some ways, they also help us understand things about our future.

UNIT 12 QUESTIONS

Name

Date

The following pages have questions based on the texts from Unit 12. You may look at the stories to help answer any questions. Use the back of the page if you need extra space for writing your answers.

1 Why is Elsa's family having a carnival?

   (a) They want to raise some money to help her family.

   (b) They like going to carnivals.

   (c) They hope to raise money for a local charity.

   (d) They want to help Elsa have a job for the summer.

2 What do both texts have in common?

   (a) paleontology

   (b) archaeology

   (c) carnivals

   (d) dinosaurs

3 How would Elsa most likely feel if her parents asked her to work a different booth?

   (a) disappointed

   (b) happy

   (c) bored

   (d) cheerful

4 Using information from the text, explain the answer you chose for #3.

_____

_____

_____

_____

5 What do paleontologists study?

   (a) fossils from the past

   (b) things found in the ocean

   (c) ancient books

   (d) things from modern times

6 Using information from the text, list two reasons why Elsa likes working at the carnival.

a. _____

_____

b. _____

_____

7 Write one sentence from the text "Job in the Dirt" that is a fact.

_____

_____

_____

8 Now that you know what paleontology is, write one opinion you have about the scientists who study fossils from the past.

_____

_____

_____

9 Why does Elsa most likely want to be a paleontologist when she grows up?

(a) She knows someone who is a paleontologist.

(b) Her family has encouraged her to become a paleontologist.

(c) She learned about paleontology from working the carnival each year.

(d) She likes playing in the dirt and sand.

10 Explain why a paleontologist would need to have a lot of patience when working.

_____

_____

_____

_____

Time to Write!

Elsa and her family hold a carnival each year. The carnival is held to raise money for a local charity. Think of someone or some group you wish you could help. Imagine you could have a fundraiser to help make money for this person or group. Use the space below to plan your event.

This is who I would help: _____.

I would make money to help them by _____

_____.

I hope they could spend the money on the following things:

_____   _____

_____   _____

_____   _____

These are the people I would ask to help me with the big event:

_____   _____

_____   _____

_____   _____

I would ask them because I know they would _____

_____.

Here is what I would plan for this big event:

_____

_____

_____

_____

_____

Trip to the Zoo

"It won't be long until we see the pandas."

Uncle David was talking to Samuel, but he barely heard him. There were so many things to see at the zoo. Samuel didn't know how his uncle expected him to see it all in one day. He told his uncle that as he caught up to him.

"I know," Uncle David said, "and I agree, Samuel, but one day is all we have. We have to meet your parents tomorrow, and then it's back to Montana for you. You also know it's time for school to start, so there is no way you can stay any extra days."

Samuel sighed. He knew his uncle was right. He was looking forward to seeing his mom and dad. The zoo was simply an amazing place. He knew the next time he visited his uncle, he would want to come here first.

Just then, Samuel and his uncle turned the corner and spotted tall plants growing everywhere. It took Samuel a moment to realize he was seeing bamboo. Then he remembered what loved bamboo: pandas. He was finally going to see his first panda!

Before he could say anything, he saw the massive creature on the other side of the habitat. The black and white fur was so unique. There was no way a person could confuse the bear with any other animal. Seeing the panda up close, Samuel could not imagine a world where pandas no longer existed. "Uncle David," Samuel said, "why are giant pandas endangered?"

"Much of their original habitat is gone. If the giant panda does not have the bamboo it needs to survive, then it will die out. That is why it is so important to preserve its habitat. It's also important for zoos, like this one, to take care of the pandas. Seeing them here reminds everyone how special they are."

The Giant Panda

The giant panda is an animal on the endangered species list. This means that without careful attention, the giant panda could become extinct. There could be a world in which no giant pandas exist. What happens to make an animal become nearly extinct?

In the case of the giant panda, the animal's habitat is slowly disappearing. Giant pandas are native to China. The giant panda eats a lot of bamboo each day. In fact, the panda can eat over eighty pounds of bamboo each day. Unfortunately for the large animals, much of China's forestland has been cut down. The bamboo no longer exists there. The main food source of the giant panda is in short supply. This makes it hard for an animal that can grow up to weigh a couple hundred pounds. If there is no food for an animal this size, the animal simply will not be able to exist any longer.

One thing many people may not know about pandas is that they are vegetarians. Their favorite food is bamboo, which grows naturally in several regions of China. However, due to the loss of forests, pandas live in only a few small areas of China. The loss of its food source, however, is not the only reason the panda has become an endangered animal. Another problem is that pandas were hunted for their unusual fur.

Today, governments in both China and the United States are trying to work together to help save the pandas. Several pandas have been placed in zoos. Hopefully, the pandas will thrive and then give birth to new pandas. This will help increase the population of the endangered animal.

One thing is certain. The loss of the panda bear to extinction should not be an option. Every effort should be made to help protect this amazing animal.

The following pages have questions based on the texts from Unit 13. You may look at the stories to help answer any questions. Use the back of the page if you need extra space for writing your answers.

1 What do the two texts have in common?

(a) pandas

(b) zoos

(c) summer

(d) China

2 Based on the text, which is true about the giant panda?

(a) They are extinct.

(b) They are dangerous.

(c) They are endangered.

(d) They are shy.

3 Write a two- to three-sentence summary of the text "Trip to the Zoo."

_____

_____

_____

_____

4 Based on your understanding of #3, explain what the word *summary* means.

_____

_____

5 Why can Samuel only spend one day at the zoo?

(a) His uncle has to go back to work.

(b) Samuel is going back to Montana.

(c) They do not have enough money for more zoo tickets.

(d) The zoo will be closed the next day.

6 Compare the giant panda to another animal you already know about. Write the name of the animal. Then list two ways they are alike.

    a. The _____ is like the panda because _____

    _____.

    b. The _____ is like the panda because _____

    _____.

7 Based on the text, what will Samuel want to do the next time he visits his uncle?

_____

_____

8 Write the sentence from the text that helped you to answer #7.

_____

_____

9 List two reasons from the text that explain why the giant panda is an endangered animal.

    a. _____

    _____

    b. _____

    _____

10 Giant pandas can be found in some zoos in the United States. Write your opinion on whether pandas should be kept in zoos. Explain your answer.

_____

_____

_____

_____

Time to Write!

It's time to do some research. With the help of your teacher, research any animal except the panda that is on the endangered species list.

Write a four- to five-sentence paragraph about the animal you research. Be sure to explain why the animal is endangered. Also, explain what is being done to save the animal.

My endangered animal is the _____.

It lives in _____.

Let me tell you some more about this special animal.

_____

_____

_____

_____

_____

_____

_____

_____

_____

_____

_____

_____

_____

_____

_____

Something Extra: On the back of the page, draw and color a picture of the endangered animal you have researched.

A Bright Idea

Hayden did not like how dark her room was when she went to bed each night. Her parents had suggested she get a nightlight. To her, the problem with a nightlight was it seemed like something a baby would use. She was not a baby. She was in the fourth grade. Still, she did not like the dark. Her mother told her some people never like the dark. She told Hayden it was perfectly fine that she wanted her room to have light even at night. Hayden knew she needed to come up with a way to give her room just a little bit of light each night. Too much light, and she knew she would not be able to sleep. Too little light, and she would be scared.

On Sunday, Hayden and her family went to visit her mother's best friend. Hayden watched as her mother pulled the car up to a large gate. She punched a series of numbers into a small box. The gate swung open. Hayden's mother drove her car through the gate down along the long drive. When Hayden asked her mother about the gate, she explained that the gate worked on a special code. Her friend gave her a code so she could enter the gate. Not everyone was given a code to the gate. Hayden wondered how the gate worked. She did not see any electrical wires powering the large structure.

Once they arrived at the house and everyone said their hellos, Hayden asked Mrs. Brown a question. She wanted to know how the gate worked without electricity. Mrs. Brown explained that the gate worked using solar power. Hayden listened to Mrs. Brown. Then she had an idea. She knew what she was going to do to solve the problem of her light. She would invent a light that did not look like a nightlight. She could keep the light by her bed each night, but each day she would put the special light outside. The sun would charge the light, so it would not need to use electricity. Hayden would not feel bad about keeping her light on all night because she would be using the solar power she had collected during the day. She would still need to do some research on the best way to build the light, but at least she now knew how she would power her new invention.

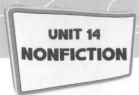

Inventors are people who have amazing ideas. Many of their ideas have changed the world for the better. Imagine a world without zippers! Or imagine never being able to watch a movie! Inventions can change a person's world.

For an invention to be a success, the inventor must come up with an idea that other people want or can use. An inventor might also want to obtain a patent for his or her invention. A patent is an official document from the government. These documents can be given to people who apply for them. So why would someone want a patent? There are two main reasons. When someone invents something he or she wants to sell, he or she wants to make sure no one else has already invented the same thing. He or she does not want to try and take credit for anyone else's ideas. If an inventor gets a patent, it also protects his or her idea from other people. With a patent, no one can take his or her invention, and he or she can sell the idea to try to make money.

Not all inventions need a patent. If there is only a small change in a product, it does not need a patent. When the size or color of an invention changes, it does not need a patent either. For example, if someone invented a new type of toaster, he or she might want to get a patent. If someone changed the color of the toaster from red to blue, then that is not a big change. Finally, if an invention is not useful, there is no reason to try to get a patent.

Could someone your age or younger get a patent for an invention? Yes! In fact, the youngest person to ever receive a patent was only four years old. Her name was Sydney Dittman. She invented a tool that helps people open drawers and cabinets. Sydney is not the only young inventor. There have been many more. Many young people enter contests to help get their ideas noticed. As most inventors find out, getting a patent is not an easy process. It takes much time and money. This does not mean people should ever give up. Just think about a world with no music or electric lights! We all owe so much to the amazing minds of inventors.

UNIT 14 QUESTIONS

Name _____ **Date** _____

The following pages have questions based on the texts from Unit 14. You may look at the stories to help answer any questions. Use the back of the page if you need extra space for writing your answers.

1 What is Hayden's problem each night?

   (a) Her room is too light.

   (b) There is so much noise, she can't sleep.

   (c) She has bad dreams each night.

   (d) Her room is too dark.

2 What do both texts have in common?

   (a) They are both about facing a person's fears.

   (b) They are both about inventions.

   (c) They are both about playing outside.

   (d) They are both about getting a patent for an invention.

3 Which is true about getting a patent?

   (a) Anyone can get a patent at any age.

   (b) Only adults can get patents.

   (c) A patent is a free document given by the government.

   (d) A patent can be given for any invention.

4 Which sentence best describes Hayden?

   (a) She is scared.

   (b) She is shy.

   (c) She is creative.

   (d) She is lazy.

5 Write one sentence to explain how Hayden will make her light work.

_____

_____

_____

_____

6 Which paragraph from the text "Inventions" best explains what a patent is?

     (a) paragraph 1

     (b) paragraph 2

     (c) paragraph 3

     (d) paragraph 4

7 How can inventions change a person's world? Give a specific example and explain your choice.

_____

_____

_____

8 List three events in chronological order that happened in the text "A Bright Idea."

     a. _____

       _____

     b. _____

       _____

     c. _____

       _____

9 Which statement would Hayden most likely agree with?

     (a) Everyone can make a difference.

     (b) No one should be afraid of the dark.

     (c) Summer is the best season.

     (d) Friends are forever.

10 Explain why you chose the answer you did for #9. Use an example from the text to support your answer choice.

_____

_____

Time to Write!

All great inventions begin with someone's great idea. Think of a great idea of your own, and create a new invention that can be used at school. To help you begin, think of something that you can improve at school. Think about how your invention can be useful to you or to other people. Use the space below to describe your new invention.

My new invention is called _____.

This invention is needed at school. This is how it can be used: _____

_____

_____

_____

This is how I will make my invention: _____

_____

_____

_____

Here is a picture of my invention:

The Hidden House

The tree's branch was just low enough that Emily could see what was there. A small nest was hidden among the leaves. Emily tried to look closer without disrupting the nest. She was tall enough to see the nest, but she was not tall enough to see if anything was inside it.

Heading back to her home, Emily kept wondering what was in the nest. The tree sat at the back of her yard. If there were baby birds or even still eggs in the nest, she really wanted to know. She knew she wasn't supposed to touch a baby bird. She did not want to bother the eggs. What she did want was to keep anything else from bothering the hidden bird's house. If she found out there was something in the nest, she would spend much of her time looking after the precious cargo.

Emily told her father about her problem. Her dad suggested she take a small stool outside. The stool had three steps. It usually stayed in the kitchen. Emily used the stool whenever she needed to reach the top shelves in a cabinet. The stool was made of sturdy plastic, so her father assured her it would not get ruined in the yard.

Emily gave her father a quick hug. She grabbed the stool and headed back out to the tree. Her father had warned her to be extra careful. He reminded her that a mother bird would not understand why she was there. The bird would not know she only wanted to help.

Another idea came to Emily. She ran back to the house and found a pair of binoculars she had used at camp one year. With the binoculars, she would not have to get as close to the nest. Emily climbed up the three short steps. She raised the binoculars, to her eyes so she could see better, and then she smiled.

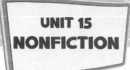

Animal Houses

All animals need a place to call home. Their homes help keep them safe and give them shelter when they need it. Like people, all animals do not have the same types of homes. An animal's habitat must fit the needs of the specific animal. This is why each animal's home is as unique as it is. If you pay close attention when you are outside, you just might see the homes of some animals. A bird might be found in its nest. A raccoon might be seen in the hollowed out trunk of a tree. A spider might be seen sitting on its web. Some animals carry their homes with them. Certain types of sea creatures carry their shells as they move along.

One type of animal home you might not notice are the burrows that are under the ground. Moles, rabbits, and other creatures dig tunnels underneath the earth. They can escape the heat in their underground houses. They can also escape predators that want to have them for lunch! Most burrows have two different ways in and out. This special feature keeps the animal safe.

Turtles and tortoises also have special homes. In fact, they carry their homes with them wherever they travel. They can keep themselves safe by using the homes they have with them all the time. Whenever a predator tries to hurt one of these creatures, they simply pull their bodies inside their homes. By retreating into the hard shells on their backs, they are using their houses for protection against predators.

There is one other type of home for animals that is not as fun as all the rest. Some creatures make you their home! Tics like to become attached to human hosts. They live off the person to whom they are attached. Lice like to make their homes in the hairs on the tops of people's heads. Fleas are another creature that make their homes where they are not wanted. They enjoy finding their hidden spot among the fur on your dog's or cat's body.

There are many different types of animals and many different types of homes. Just try to make sure that you aren't home to too many creatures!

UNIT 15 QUESTIONS

Name _____ **Date** _____

The following pages have questions based on the texts from Unit 15. You may look at the stories to help answer any questions. Use the back of the page if you need extra space for writing your answers.

1 Why is the text titled "The Hidden House"?

ⓐ because the nest is hidden in the tree

ⓑ because the nest is nearly invisible

ⓒ because the nest has a covering over the top

ⓓ because the nest is on top of the ladder

2 Why does Emily need advice from her father?

ⓐ She needs to ask him where she can find a ladder.

ⓑ She needs to ask him if she can have a baby bird for a pet.

ⓒ She needs to ask him how she can see into the nest.

ⓓ She needs to ask him where she can get a pair of binoculars.

3 According to the nonfiction text, list two ways an animal's home is important to the animal.

a. _____

b. _____

4 Based on what you have read, which is NOT a true statement about the homes of animals.

ⓐ Each animal's home fits the needs of the individual animal.

ⓑ An animal's home can never be moved.

ⓒ Animals can use their homes to help keep them safe.

ⓓ An animal's home might be above or below the ground.

5 Think of a type of animal not mentioned in either text. Write the name of the animal and explain how its home helps keep it safe.

_____

_____

_____

_____

6 Write two to three sentences summarizing the text "The Hidden House."

_____

_____

_____

_____

7 Explain why Emily is smiling at the end of the text "The Hidden House."

_____

_____

8 Why do some animals make their homes on other living creatures?

_____

_____

9 Write the name of the animal from the text that lives in each home shown below.

_____   _____   _____

10 Write a prediction about what you think Emily found once she was able to see inside the nest.

_____

_____

Time to Write!

Imagine there are several acres of woods near your school. The city's mayor wants to clear the land to build a park for your school.

Write a letter to the city's newspaper trying to persuade the city not to clear the area. Your major concern is the loss of habitat for the creatures that live in the woods. Give at least three reasons why you do not believe the area should be cleared for a playground.

Dear Mayor,

_____

_____

_____

_____

_____

_____

_____

_____

_____

_____

_____

Sincerely,

_____

The Winner

"On your mark, get set, go!" The announcer's voice came loud and clear across the speaker. On the word "go," ten athletes from ten different schools began their competition. The race was on! Young student athletes began to run toward the finish line. The competition was exciting.

Cole watched from the sidelines. This was his brother's first time to compete in the Special Olympics. Cole's school was hosting the event, and all of the students had been allowed to come outside and watch the exciting competitions. Cole was happy to see his brother in the competition. He loved running, and he knew even if Andrew didn't win, he would still have a great day. He and Cole raced all the time. Andrew was fast. He beat Cole many times when they raced at home. Cole just didn't know how many of the other competitors were faster than his brother. He guessed they would all know soon.

As the race ended, Cole rushed to the finish line to find his brother. Andrew was there. He was bent over at the waist and breathing hard. When he raised his head, he was grinning. He had won second place. He had a silver medal. Cole was so proud of his brother. He knew he had done his very best.

When Andrew received his medal, Cole asked for permission to take a picture. He snapped the picture and sent it to his dad. He knew his father would be so proud of Andrew. Cole wished his father could have been here to see Andrew race, but his father was away on a business trip. Cole knew his dad would want all the details of the race when he returned. He knew Andrew would love telling the story over and over again.

Cole looked at the schedule. Andrew would not have another event for at least thirty minutes. That would give him plenty of time to call his grandparents and tell them to start cooking. They had promised Andrew a special dinner tonight just for competing. The fact that Andrew had won a silver medal would make the dinner even better.

A Special Competition

Many people love to compete at sports. People with special needs can play and compete in a program known as the Special Olympics. These Olympic Games give people a chance to compete as athletes.

The founder of the Special Olympics was Eunice Kennedy Shriver. Eunice's sister had an intellectual disability. When John F. Kennedy became president, Eunice knew her brother could help. She began to help make people more aware about people with disabilities of all types.

Eunice began having camps for children and adults with disabilities. She would later help start the Special Olympics. These Games would allow people with disabilities to be able to compete in athletic events. These athletes would compete with other people from all over the world. The first international Games were held in Chicago in 1968. There are both summer and winter competitions. The Special Olympics are held every two years. Special Olympics have become a worldwide event. Countries from all around the globe host the competition. Local areas also participate in the event. Many schools and local communities have their own competitions and celebrations each year.

The Special Olympics are both fun and challenging. Many people volunteer just so they can be a part of such a special event. Everyone involved in the games is a winner.

UNIT 16 QUESTIONS

Name _____ **Date** _____

The following pages have questions based on the texts from Unit 16. You may look at the stories to help answer any questions. Use the back of the page if you need extra space for writing your answers.

1 Why is the text titled "The Winner" if Andrew did not win first place?

    (a) Andrew won first place in a different event.

    (b) Cole thought Andrew had won first place.

    (c) Cole told their father that Andrew had won first place.

    (d) Andrew is a winner because he tried his best.

2 What type of event is Andrew doing?

    (a) He is swimming.

    (b) He is running.

    (c) He is skiing.

    (d) He is bowling.

3 What do both articles have in common?

    (a) They are both about the Special Olympics.

    (b) They are both about two brothers.

    (c) They are both about winning a silver medal.

    (d) They are both about the start of the Special Olympics.

4 Why was Eunice Kennedy Shriver most likely interested in helping start the Special Olympics?

_____

_____

_____

5 Which word best describes Cole?

    (a) caring

    (b) thoughtless

    (c) friendly

    (d) stubborn

6 Write one to two sentences explaining what the Special Olympics are.

_____

_____

_____

_____

7 Which statement is an opinion?

   (a) Everyone involved in the Games is a winner whether they win a medal or not.

   (b) The first international Games were held in Chicago in 1968.

   (c) There are both summer and winter competitions.

   (d) The Special Olympics are held every two years.

8 Which will most likely happen if Andrew competes in the Special Olympics next time?

   (a) His father will be there.

   (b) He will only win a silver medal.

   (c) He will ask Cole not to be there.

   (d) He will refuse to try.

9 Explain why Mrs. Shriver's brother being president would have helped her with her idea.

_____

_____

_____

10 Explain what the word *hosting* means as it is used in the following sentence:

Cole's school was hosting the event, and all of the students had been allowed to come outside and watch the exciting competitions.

_____

_____

Time to Write!

Part 1

With your teacher's help, research some of the events that are in the Special Olympics. You can include both summer and winter events. Write what you find in the box below.

Part 2

If you could participate in the Games, which competition would you most want to do? Give at least two reasons why you would like to do this event.

I would participate in the _____.

I would do this event because _____

_____

_____.

Egyptian Wonders

"Just five more sugar cubes," Anson announced to his partner, Mia. "All we need are five more cubes, and our pyramid will be complete."

Anson and Mia had been working on their project for history class for almost a week. Their class had been studying ancient Egypt. The students had been placed into small groups. Each group was asked to create a project. Anson and Mia had teamed up. The teacher had given them permission to make a model of the Great Pyramid. Studying the Great Pyramid had taught both Anson and Mia a lot about the other pyramids in Egypt. They felt like it was taking them forever to finish their small model. They could not imagine what it must have been like to build the real pyramid.

Anson reached into the box of supplies. He looked again. Then he looked up at Mia. "There are no more sugar cubes. Where are the rest of the sugar cubes? We had plenty of cubes left yesterday."

Mia did not answer Anson. Instead, she looked down. Then she looked all around the room. Anson noticed she was looking everywhere except at him.

"Did you eat the sugar cubes?" Anson asked Mia. A bright red stain crept into her cheeks.

Mia slowly nodded. She told Anson that yesterday she'd run out of time to eat breakfast. When they were putting away the supplies, she'd realized how hungry she was. She'd eaten the sugar cubes then.

"Don't worry," Anson told her. "The stone at the top of the real Great Pyramid is missing, too! We can't lose any more stones, though. So, if you get hungry again, make sure you don't eat the ones we've already used," he laughed. "After all, they are all covered in glue!"

The Great Pyramid

The Great Pyramid of Giza is in the modern city of Cairo in Egypt. The pyramid was built sometime near 2584 B.C. The large pyramid took around twenty years to build. The ancient burial tomb is still standing today. In fact, tourists can go to Egypt to visit this amazing wonder.

In ancient Egypt, pyramids were built to be the resting places of the pharaohs of Egypt. The Great Pyramid was the burial chamber of the pharaoh Khufu. Khufu's burial chamber is not the only pyramid in the area. There are other smaller pyramids near the base of the Great Pyramid.

Pyramids were filled with items the people believed their leaders would need in their next lives. The Egyptian people believed in a life after death where people would be able to take things with them. The pyramids had secret rooms and traps to try and stop grave robbers from taking any items that were inside.

The Great Pyramid is built with four flat sides that go up to a point at the top. If you saw a picture of the ancient pyramid, you would not see the top point. Today, that stone is missing. The stones that were used to build the pyramid were big and heavy. A single stone block weighed about 2.5 tons. The entire pyramid had more than two million of these heavy stones.

There are other amazing monuments near the Great Pyramid. The Great Sphinx is also located just outside the pyramid. Some believe the statue with the human head and body of a lion acts as a guard to the tomb. However, nothing is as impressive as Khufu's final resting place. The Great Pyramid of Giza is truly one of the ancient wonders of the world.

UNIT 17 QUESTIONS

Name _____ **Date** _____

The following pages have questions based on the texts from Unit 17. You may look at the stories to help answer any questions. Use the back of the page if you need extra space for writing your answers.

1 What subject do the two texts have in common?

(a) Greece

(b) pyramids

(c) school

(d) sphinx

2 What are Anson and Mia doing?

(a) They are making a model of a spaceship.

(b) They are making a model of a Sphinx.

(c) They are making a model of a pyramid.

(d) They are making a model of a car.

3 According to the text, why was the Great Pyramid built?

(a) as a tomb for a pharaoh

(b) as a tourist attraction

(c) as a burial place for Egyptian citizens

(d) as a temple for worship

4 Explain what problem Anson and Mia have with their project.

_____

_____

_____

_____

5 Anson and Mia have the problem in #4 because

(a) Mia ate part of the supplies.

(b) Mia lost part of the supplies.

(c) Mia gave away part of the supplies.

(d) Mia took home part of the supplies.

6 Write two facts about the Great Pyramid.

_____

_____

_____

_____

7 Based on what you know of the characters, would Anson want to be partners with Mia if they were given another project? Explain your answer.

_____

_____

_____

_____

8 According to the text, what is missing from the Great Pyramid?
- **a** a way inside
- **b** the top stone
- **c** the treasures inside
- **d** stones from the base

9 If you were in Anson's place, how would you have reacted to the missing sugar cubes? Explain your answer.

_____

_____

_____

_____

10 Write one sentence from the text "The Great Pyramid" that is an opinion.

_____

_____

_____

_____

Time to Write!

The pharaohs of ancient Egypt believed they should prepare for a long trip after their death. They put inside their tombs things they did not want to leave behind.

Imagine you are going on a long trip away from your home. You can only take four things with you. The four things cannot be people or pets. You will also have plenty of clothes and food where you are going. You do not have to take those things with you.

Think about what four things you would take with you that won't already be where you are going. Use the space below (and the back, if needed) to write about what you are taking and why.

I will take the following things with me on my trip:

1. _____

   I will take this because _____

   _____.

2. _____

   I will take this because _____

   _____.

3. _____

   I will take this because _____

   _____.

4. _____

   I will take this because _____

   _____.

Jackie was going to see her father. Each summer, she would go and stay with him until school began again. Her father lived in a different state than Jackie did. Jackie lived the rest of the year with her mother. She loved going to see her dad. He lived in Florida. When she went to see him, she could go to the beach. She could play in the ocean. She could search for shells. The only thing she didn't like was the long drive to get to her father's house, but this year she was doing something new. She was flying to Florida.

A few weeks earlier, Jackie's father had called and talked to her mother. The conversation went on for a long time. Jackie wondered what they were talking about for so long. She knew it had something to do with her, but she did not know what. When her mother hung up the phone, she told Jackie she wanted to talk to her. Jackie listened as her mother explained that a new airport had been built just minutes from where her father lived. Jackie's father had called to ask if Jackie could fly down to see him. Jackie's mother thought the trip would be easier on her because it would be so much shorter. She was worried, though, about Jackie flying. She had never flown before, and if she went, she would have to fly by herself. Both parents agreed they would let Jackie decide.

Jackie thought about it all night and all the next day. Finally, she made up her mind. She wanted to fly. She wanted to know what it was like to be high above the ground. She told her mother she would be fine. She was excited about the idea. She also told her mother she wanted a window seat so she could look outside while they were flying.

Now it was the big day. Jackie wasn't sure how she was feeling about the trip. She was nervous and excited all at the same time. She hoped everything would go okay once she got on the plane. Once Jackie decided to fly to her dad's, she started studying everything she could about the history of flight. She knew a lot of people were involved in making flight possible. Jackie knew she wasn't going to be the first person ever to fly like Wilbur Wright, but she bet she knew exactly how he felt the first time he did!

Twelve Seconds of Change

For centuries, people would look at the birds in the sky and wonder what it would be like to fly. The desire to fly in the sky would not end for some people. They believed humans could fly. Orville and Wilbur Wright were two brothers who believed in this dream. The two brothers wanted to build a successful flying machine. They believed it was possible for people to fly. The two brothers did many experiments with flight. Some were not as successful as others. However, with each flight experiment, they learned new things. Even their flights that were failures taught them new things about how to build their flying machine.

The Wright brothers' design for a machine that could fly did not look like a modern-day airplane. The glider they used did have a motor, but it had no wheels for landing like modern-day planes do. The wings were not made of any type of metal. Instead, they were framed from wood and covered with cloth. There was a propeller on the glider. It was also made from wood.

Have you ever heard the expression, "If at first you don't succeed, then try, try again?" The Wright brothers did just that. They attempted to fly more than 250 times. They wanted their engine-powered flyer to be a success. The two brothers refused to give up.

Since the Wright brothers' flying machine had no wheels for landing, the brothers liked to use the sandy beaches of South Carolina's shores as a place to experiment with their machine. The soft sand was a good place to work. On December 17, 1903, the Wright brothers were at the beach near Kitty Hawk, South Carolina. Not only did the spot have lots of sand, but the winds from the sea were perfect. On that day in December, the two brothers decided to flip a coin to see who would try to fly first. Wilbur won the toss. Orville would also fly later that same day. For the first time, the brothers had complete success. The *Flyer* left the ground. Wilbur Wright was flying! He only stayed in the air for twelve seconds. Yet, those twelve seconds helped change the world.

UNIT 18
QUESTIONS

Name _____ **Date** _____

The following pages have questions based on the texts from Unit 18. You may look at the stories to help answer any questions. Use the back of the page if you need extra space for writing your answers.

1 In the fiction text, what does Jackie not like about going to her father's house?

- (a) leaving her mother
- (b) the long drive
- (c) the hot temperatures
- (d) staying all summer

2 Write the sentence from the text that helped you to answer #1.

_____

_____

_____

_____

3 On December 17, 1903, why was Wilbur flying the plane that stayed in the air instead of Orville?

- (a) Wilbur was older than Orville.
- (b) Wilbur asked Orville to let him pilot the glider first.
- (c) Wilbur jumped in the glider first.
- (d) The two brothers flipped a coin to see who would go first.

4 List two ways the Wright brothers' flying machine was different than an airplane of today.

a. _____

b. _____

5 What would be a good alternative title for the text "Twelve Seconds of Change"? Why would this be a good alternative?

_____

_____

_____

6 Write one way Jackie and the Wright brothers are alike.

_____

_____

7 Why does Jackie want a window seat?

    (**a**) so she can look outside during the flight

    (**b**) so she does not have to sit near the aisle

    (**c**) so she can take pictures

    (**d**) so she can wave to her mother when she is leaving

8 Give an example of something you have tried to do but were not good at the first time. Did you try again? Why or why not?

_____

_____

_____

_____

_____

9 Which statement is true about the Wright Brothers and their flight?

    (**a**) The flight lasted only twenty seconds.

    (**b**) The brothers fought over who would fly the glider.

    (**c**) The Wright brothers' flying machine had no wheels for landing.

    (**d**) Orville Wright never had a chance to fly the glider.

10 Think for a minute about flying. Have you flown anywhere? If yes, how did flying make you feel? If no, would you ever want to fly? Explain your answer.

_____

_____

_____

_____

Time to Write!

Orville and Wilbur Wright had a dream to fly. They helped make that dream come true for many people. Today, people don't always fly only in planes. One other way people can travel high in the sky is by riding in a hot-air balloon.

Think about dreams you have that you hope will come true. Write at least one of your dreams in the basket of the hot-air balloon. Color the balloon when you are finished writing.

Finally, use the back of the page to write about a way you can make this dream come true.

The sun was bright in the sky. Birds were everywhere. The clouds were big, white, and fluffy. The day was picture perfect, but it didn't feel that way to Thomas. He was not happy, and his attitude made the entire day seem dark and dreary.

"Thomas," his mother said, "there is no reason to frown. This is not a bad thing."

Thomas would not answer her.

"The doctor said getting glasses would help you. You have been having trouble seeing things for a long time. Having glasses will make things so clear for you. You will be able to see the board from your seat. You won't have to sit in the front row anymore. Getting glasses will be a good thing. You'll see."

Thomas let out a loud sigh. "No one will want to vote for me as class president," he said. "No one else in my grade wears glasses. Why can't I get contact lenses?"

"Oh, Thomas," his mother said, "you heard what the eye doctor said. Contacts will not work with the eye condition you have. I think you are wrong to say no one will vote for you for president because you have something about you that is different. People will vote for who you are inside."

Thomas's mother could tell he wanted to believe her, but he wasn't sure. "Franklin Delano Roosevelt is the perfect example," she began. "He had polio. Polio is a disease you get a vaccine for now, so you don't have to worry about getting it, Thomas. However, when Roosevelt lived, anyone could get the disease. The disease left him partially paralyzed. He did not let that stop him. He went on to become the president of the United States."

Thomas knew his mother was right. He should be glad he was getting glasses that would help him. If Mr. Roosevelt could be president of a country, he could be president of his class.

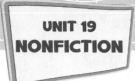

Mr. President

Franklin Delano Roosevelt was born in 1882, in New York. He would later grow up to become the president of the United States. He would be the only president ever elected to office for four terms.

Roosevelt was an only child. His family was very wealthy. He had a good childhood. When he got older, he went to college. He decided he wanted to be a politician. Politicians are people who run for office so they can help their cities, states, or countries. He decided he wanted to become a senator for his state. He ran for office, and he won. He also met and married Eleanor Roosevelt. His entire life seemed to be going perfectly.

In 1921, something terrible happened to Roosevelt. He became ill. At first, none of the doctors knew what was wrong with him. Finally, one of the doctors told him he had polio. Today, people are able to get a vaccine so they will not get polio, but when Roosevelt got sick, there was no vaccine for the virus. The virus caused Roosevelt to become paralyzed. At the age of thirty-nine, Roosevelt could no longer walk unless someone was helping him.

Roosevelt's disease made him more determined than ever to help other people in need. He bought land in a place called Warm Springs, Georgia. The land had natural springs of water. The water was supposed to help people feel better. The Roosevelts invited people to come use the healing waters. Franklin Roosevelt also hired people to work there to help find cures or treatments for his disease.

Roosevelt did not let his polio stop him from reaching his goals. He became governor of his state, and in 1933, he became the president of the country. While Roosevelt was president, the country would go through many struggles, including the Great Depression and World War II. Roosevelt never doubted that he could do whatever he decided to do.

The following pages have questions based on the texts from Unit 19. You may look at the stories to help answer any questions. Use the back of the page if you need extra space for writing your answers.

1 Why is Thomas upset?

    (a) He has to get braces.

    (b) He failed a test at school.

    (c) He dropped out of the race for class president.

    (d) He has to get glasses.

2 Write a sentence explaining what Thomas and Franklin Delano Roosevelt have in common.

_____

_____

_____

3 What will Thomas most likely do when he goes back to school?

    (a) He will run for class president.

    (b) He will no longer run for class president.

    (c) He will ask his best friend to run for class president.

    (d) He will not wear his glasses when he goes back to school.

4 What happened to Franklin Roosevelt when he got polio?

    (a) He lost his voice.

    (b) His lost his eyesight.

    (c) He lost the use of his legs.

    (d) He lost his hearing.

5 Write the sentence or sentences from the text that helped you to answer #4.

_____

_____

_____

6 What does Thomas's decision to still run for class president tell you about him?

_____

_____

_____

7 Which adjective best describes both Thomas and Franklin Roosevelt?

(a) lazy

(b) determined

(c) kind

(d) loyal

8 Using information from the texts, explain why you chose the answer you did for #7.

_____

_____

_____

_____

9 What does the title of the text "Seeing Things Clearly" mean?

_____

_____

_____

10 In the text, Thomas is told that people now get a vaccine so they will not get polio. What does the word _vaccine_ mean?

_____

_____

_____

Time to Write!

Imagine you are running for class president. Write a speech to persuade the people in your class to vote for you. List at least three reasons why you would be a great class president.

_____

_____

_____

_____

_____

_____

_____

_____

_____

_____

_____

_____

_____

_____

_____

_____

_____

_____

Something Extra: On the back of the page, draw a poster for your campaign. Be sure to include a great picture and some of the reasons why you should be class president.

The Show

Tamara and her sister Jana were sitting with their grandparents in the front row. Their grandparents had bought them tickets to a nighttime dolphin show. The girls loved to visit the local aquarium whenever they visited their grandparents. Until today, they had never bought tickets to go to the show. They could not believe they had front-row tickets. They both loved dolphins.

Because of the many trips to the aquarium, Tamara wanted to be a marine biologist when she grew up. She wanted to study animals that live in the water. She wanted to make sure that the animals were safe. Tamara hoped that someday she could help make sure water habitats were safe for all creatures that lived in the ocean.

Jana loved coming to the aquarium, too. She was not like Tamara. Jana was always nervous whenever they were too close to the animals. The dolphins were different to Jana. They always seemed like such gentle creatures. The only time they scared her was when their fins were the only thing she could see. Then they reminded her of sharks.

Tamara was so glad Jana loved the dolphins as much as she did. Tamara knew that part of the fun of the show was being able to share it with her family. She wished her parents could have been here, too. She knew they would love to see the dolphins, but they both had to work.

The lights began to dim. A spotlight appeared above the tank. The crowd grew quiet. Tamara could hear the familiar clicking noise of the dolphins as they came into view. One came close to the edge of the tank. It flipped water right at Jana. The girls clapped loudly. Tamara could already tell this was going to be a night she would never forget.

Dolphins are mammals, not fish. Unlike fish, dolphins need to breathe air to survive. They use the blowhole on top of their heads to help them take in and release air. Dolphins don't just need air to survive. They also need water to live. The ocean is the perfect place for these amazing creatures.

A dolphin has special fins that help it to be a great swimmer. The dolphin also has two flippers that help with balance. The dolphin's mighty tail fin is called a *fluke*. This powerful fin helps the dolphin glide easily through the water. In captivity, people can train dolphins to appear to walk on water. The dolphins come up almost all the way out of the water. Then they use their tail fins or flukes to help them stay upright.

Some people have been lucky enough to hear a dolphin make a clicking noise. A dolphin uses this noise to make an echo in the water. The sound the dolphin makes can travel through the water in waves. If the sound hits something in its path, it will bounce back to the dolphin. This helps the dolphin know if food or a predator might be in its path. This special location system is called *echolocation*. People who study dolphins believe the clicking sounds are also a way dolphins communicate. Many people believe the different noises mean different things to other dolphins. Of course, no one knows for sure what all the different sounds mean. One thing scientists have observed is how dolphins use special noises to locate other dolphins. A mother dolphin can create a unique whistle noise that her baby knows. The young dolphin can actually whistle back. This exchange of sound helps the mother dolphin keep track of her baby.

Dolphins are amazing animals. Scientists will continue to study them. Maybe someday they will learn how to clearly communicate with these marvelous creatures.

The following pages have questions based on the texts from Unit 20. You may look at the stories to help answer any questions. Use the back of the page if you need extra space for writing your answers.

1 What does the title "The Show" mean?

_____

_____

_____

2 What do the two texts have in common?

(a) Both are about fish.

(b) Both are about aquariums.

(c) Both are about the ocean.

(d) Both are about dolphins.

3 Why do dolphins need to breathe air?

(a) They are mammals.

(b) They are fish.

(c) They are amphibians.

(d) They are poor swimmers.

4 What is a dolphin's tail fin called?

(a) flipper

(b) fluke

(c) spike

(d) dorsal

5 Using information from the text, write one reason why the dolphin's tail fin is so important.

_____

_____

_____

6 Write two words that best describe Tamara.

a. _____

b. _____

7 Explain why you chose the words you did for #6.

_____

_____

8 Compare a dolphin to another animal. Write two ways the animals are the same.
Write one way they are different.

Animal: _____

Same

a. _____

b. _____

Different

a. _____

9 What would be a good alternative title for the text "Dolphins"? Why would this be a
good alternative?

_____

_____

_____

_____

10 What does the word *captivity* mean as it is used in the following sentence?

In captivity, people can train dolphins to appear to walk on water.

_____

_____

Time to Write!

Part 1

A preposition is a word that shows position. Examples of prepositions are the words *over* and *under*.

- The dolphin went over the wave.
- The dolphin went under the water.

Write four more prepositions on the dolphins that are drawn below.

Part 2

Use the four prepositions you wrote above in a story. Follow these directions when writing your story:

- One of the characters in the story should be a dolphin.
- Circle the prepositions you use.

Use the back of the page if you need more space.

_____

_____

_____

_____

_____

Lucas wished the temperature was warmer. The electricity had been off for almost eight hours. The house was starting to get cold. Lucas's father had built a fire in the fireplace in the living room. The heat from the flames felt warm to his outstretched hands. His mother had brought out blankets for Lucas and his little sister, Ann, to wrap around them. Even with the extra layers of clothes, Lucas was beginning to feel cold. Lucas knew his sister was probably feeling the cold, too. She was so much smaller than he was. He hoped she would be okay. He would give her his blanket if she needed it.

"I have a surprise for everyone!" Lucas's mother said. "I've made hot chocolate." Everyone was surprised. Lucas wondered how his mother had made hot chocolate. She passed each one of them a cup. The first sip was delicious to taste. It also made Lucas feel warm as he drank it. His little sister was letting the steam from the cup warm her face between each sip. Everyone looked happy to have their hot, tasty treat.

"Mom, how did you make our cocoa without any electricity?"

She quickly explained. "You know, Lucas, long ago people didn't have electricity. They managed to live without it for years and years. They also cooked without electricity. When I was a little girl, my grandmother used to make me hot chocolate just like I made for you. People had to adapt to survive. When the weather was cold, they had to adapt to those conditions, too. I just adapted how I cook."

"I still don't get it," Lucas's little sister spoke up.

"I do!" Lucas exclaimed. "You cooked our hot chocolate over a fire, didn't you?"

"That's right, Lucas. Your father made me a small fire in the fireplace in the kitchen. I didn't want to make the hot drinks in this fire because I wanted to surprise both of you."

"It was a great surprise, Mom," Lucas answered. His sister nodded her agreement. Lucas wasn't sure if he felt warm inside from the hot chocolate or because he knew his mom loved them all so much.

Animals Survive

People have learned to adapt to change. Modern inventions have helped people to have easier lives. Hot weather is rarely a bother when people have air conditioning. Pipes bring water into our homes, making getting a drink easy to do. Cold weather isn't a problem when people can layer up their clothes or turn on their heat. There are so many ways people have made living easier. Like people, animals must survive different temperatures. There are many different animals in the world. Some animals live in extremely cold areas. These animals have all developed ways to help them survive in the habitats where they live.

Some climates where animals live are cold. Animals have to be able to survive the extremely low temperatures. The polar bear is an example of an animal that is able to handle very cold weather. Did you know that polar bears are excellent swimmers? It is hard to imagine anything wanting to swim in the cold ocean waters where the Arctic weather causes giant icebergs. Yet, the polar bear loves to do just that. What keeps the polar bear warm while it swims? The thick fur helps, but the bear also has a layer of fat that helps keep its body temperature warm, even when it is soaking wet.

Brown bears can also survive cold winters. These bears survive cold weather by taking naps. Actually, they take very long naps. They nap through the entire winter! This is called *hibernation*. The bear eats an abundance of food before hibernating. Then, after the cold temperatures have passed, it wakes from its sleep. It has lived off the food in its body during its hibernation. Also, the food it has eaten is turned into fat. The layer of fat keeps it warm while it is hibernating.

Some of you may wish you could swim in the winter or sleep through the cold months. People adapt in other ways to cold temperatures. One thing that makes all animals special, including people, is the ability to adapt and survive extreme weather conditions.

UNIT 21
QUESTIONS

Name

Date

The following pages have questions based on the texts from Unit 21. You may look at the stories to help answer any questions. Use the back of the page if you need extra space for writing your answers.

1 Which is true about the nonfiction text?

(a) No animal can survive cold temperatures.

(b) Animals are able to adapt to many different types of weather.

(c) Only polar bears can survive extremely cold temperatures.

(d) Nothing can live outside in snow.

2 In the fiction text, why are Lucas and his family cold?

(a) They do not have enough coats.

(b) Lucas's mother forgot how to make hot chocolate.

(c) The electricity is not working.

(d) There is a blizzard at their house.

3 Write the sentence from the text that helped you to answer #2.

_____

_____

_____

_____

4 What do the two texts have in common?

(a) Both are about adapting to the weather.

(b) Both are about surviving in the Arctic.

(c) Both are about the seasons.

(d) Both are about hibernation.

5 Which paragraph explains how the brown bear adapts to the cold?

(a) paragraph 1

(b) paragraph 2

(c) paragraph 3

(d) paragraph 4

6 Write the name of an animal that can survive hot weather conditions. Write two ways this animal adapts to the hot weather.

Animal: _____

    a. _____

    b. _____

7 Based on information from the texts, write two ways people adapt to cold weather.

    a. _____

    b. _____

8 Write one reason why a bear would hibernate through the winter.

_____

_____

_____

9 Which word best describes Lucas's mother?

    (a) energetic

    (b) scared

    (c) loving

    (d) nervous

10 Explain why you chose the answer you did for #9.

_____

_____

_____

_____

Time to Write!

Part 1

Use the space below to create your very own new animal! The animal can be from your imagination, or you can combine other animals to make your new creature. An example might be a bear and a giraffe put together to become a "girear." What about mixing a cat with a rabbit? You just made the first "cabbit"!

Use this space to write the name of your new animal.

My animal is a _____.

Part 2

Answer the following questions about your animal.

1. Where does your animal live?

   _____

2. What does your animal do to adapt to its environment?

   _____

   _____

3. What predators bother your animal?

   _____

   _____

4. What does your animal eat?

   _____

   _____

5. Describe your animal.

   _____

   _____

6. Describe the place where your animal sleeps.

   _____

   _____

Something Extra: On the back of the page, write a letter to a zoo asking it to start an exhibit with your animal. Explain why the zoo needs the animal. Explain how this would be good for the zoo and the animal.

"Well, we're on our way!" Aaron's father looked over at his son. Aaron was sitting in the front seat beside his father. It was just the two of them on this trip. Aaron's dad liked for them to take trips together. Aaron did, too. They had been on camping trips. They had gone to ball games together. They had even spent a weekend visiting several different museums. This trip was as unique as all the others. They were going to Graceland. Aaron's dad had explained that Graceland was in Memphis, Tennessee. It was only a few hours from where they lived. It had been the home of the famous singer Elvis Presley. Aaron knew that Elvis had died but that he lived on through his songs. Aaron's parents were huge fans of Elvis's music. In fact, Aaron had been named after the King of Rock and Roll. Elvis's middle name was Aaron!

"Can we listen to some of Elvis's music as we travel?" Aaron asked his father. His father agreed. Aaron turned on the music. Elvis's voice filled the car. Both Aaron and his father sang along with the songs. The time seemed to fly by. Before they knew it, they had arrived at Graceland. They purchased their tickets and began the tour. As they paused in one of the rooms, the tour guide began to talk about the types of music that had influenced Elvis. Aaron listened as the guide explained that gospel music and the blues were both types of music that Elvis enjoyed. Aaron knew that gospel music was music he had learned from church. Aaron did not know what the blues were.

When the tour was over and Aaron and his father were back in the car, Aaron remembered his question. He asked his dad about the blues. Aaron's dad explained that the blues is a type of music in which people sing about their feelings and sad things. The music started in America when slaves brought from Africa would sing in the fields. They would sing about wanting to be free and hoping they could go home someday. The music, Aaron's father explained, was a way for people to express themselves. Aaron liked the blues music they had heard on the tour. He wished he could sing the blues. He knew he couldn't today. He was having too much fun to think anymore about the blues.

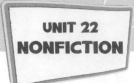
The Blues

Anyone who has ever listened to music knows there are many different types. Some people like to listen to only one type. Some people like lots of different styles of music. Music is often used as a way for people to express how they feel. When people feel happy, they might listen to songs with fast rhythms. When people are tired, they might listen to music that is calm and slow. One style of music that expresses a lot of emotions is a music style called the blues. Have you ever heard someone ask if you have "the blues"? When people ask this question, they want to know if you are sad. Blues music began as a way for people to show their emotions when they were feeling down and needed hope.

Where did the music known as the blues begin? The first recorded blues song did not happen until the early 1900s. However, people have been singing the blues for a much longer time. The words and the rhythm express or show how people sometimes feel. When people first came to America, they began colonies. Slave traders took people from their homes in Africa. They brought them by ship to the colonies. They sold these people as slaves. Most of the people who became slaves were from West Africa. They did not want to come to America. They did not want to be slaves. They wanted to be free. They wanted to go home. They showed their feelings in their music.

As the colonies grew, more slaves were brought to America. Slaves were forced to work in the fields to help grow crops. As the slaves worked, they would sing songs. The songs would involve many voices. Many of the slaves also sang spiritual songs. They would sing these songs in worship. The music that is called the blues was born from these different types of songs.

Since people began singing the blues, there have been many famous blues singers and musicians. B.B. King and Billie Holiday are two famous blues artists. Today, people still perform the blues. The soulful sound has been around for hundreds of years and will continue to be for many more.

The following pages have questions based on the texts from Unit 22. You may look at the stories to help answer any questions. Use the back of the page if you need extra space for writing your answers.

1 Where are Aaron and his father going?

- (a) on a trip to a museum
- (b) on a camping trip
- (c) to a baseball game
- (d) to Graceland

2 Who first began singing the blues?

- (a) Billie Holiday
- (b) Elvis Presley
- (c) slaves from Africa
- (d) early colonists

3 Which word best describes "the blues"?

- (a) happiness
- (b) sadness
- (c) joyfulness
- (d) loneliness

4 Where did slaves do much of their singing?

- (a) while working in the fields
- (b) while traveling on the ship
- (c) during the late hours of the night
- (d) during the early hours of the morning

5 Using what you know from the text, explain why the slaves sang as they worked.

_____

_____

_____

6 What do Aaron and Elvis have in common?

(a) Aaron plays the guitar like Elvis did.

(b) They both have "Aaron" in their name.

(c) Elvis and Aaron were born in the same state.

(d) They both like to sing and dance.

7 What does it mean when people ask if someone has "the blues"?

_____

_____

_____

8 What do the two texts have in common?

(a) Both are about blues music.

(b) Both are about Elvis Presley.

(c) Both are about spending time with family.

(d) Both are about Billie Holiday.

9 Explain why Aaron says he cannot sing the blues.

_____

_____

_____

10 Give an example of someone who uses music to show how he or she feels.

_____

_____

_____

_____

_____

Time to Write!

With your teacher's help, listen to some examples of blues music. Pay attention to how the words and music show how the singer is feeling. Write the names of the songs on the lines.

_____

_____

_____

_____

Use the space below to write your own blues song. Write a song showing how "blue" you feel about a huge homework assignment you have to do. Not only do you have a huge assignment, but you have to work over the weekend because it is due on Monday!

Show your emotions. Write the words to your song in the space below. Be ready to share your song lyrics with other people in the class.

_____

_____

_____

_____

_____

_____

_____

_____

_____

_____

_____

Signs of the Past

The car moved quickly down the road. Leeann and her mother would stop every so often to take pictures. Then they would get back in the car and drive some more. Leeann's mother was a photographer and a writer. She was creating a book about the landmark signs along the highways. Leeann had asked to go with her mother to watch her take the pictures. She had enjoyed spending the day with her mother. She liked reading the signs and learning about the history in her state.

Leeann's mother guided the car off the main road. The side street had no traffic. She invited Leeann to get out of the car with her. This time, she handed Leeann the camera. Leeann focused the camera on the sign. She snapped the picture. Her mother looked at what she had done and told her it was perfect. Then she began to read the sign out loud. Leeann listened as her mother read the words, explaining that the marker was to remind everyone about the Trail of Tears.

Leeann had never heard about this trail. She listened as her mother explained to her that the trail was walked by the Cherokee Indians. The Cherokee people had been forced to walk the trail and to leave their homes. The United States government had made them move, so settlers could take their land. Her mother went on to explain that many of the people had died as they marched west. That is why the sign calls it the Trail of Tears.

Leeann felt sad after hearing her mother read the sign. She did not understand why people had been forced to leave their homes. She wished it had not happened. She had always admired her mother. She liked that she was a writer. Now she was also very proud of her mother. Because of her mother's book, maybe more people would learn about the Trail of Tears. Maybe they would remember what happened to the Cherokee Indians. As they climbed back into the car, Leeann knew the picture she had taken was very important. She hoped people would read the sign in her mother's book and learn from the past, so no one would ever have to suffer like that again.

The Trail of Tears

Before other people came to North America, the Cherokee Indians were one of many tribes that lived on the continent. The Cherokee lived in the area that is now part of Virginia, West Virginia, Kentucky, Tennessee, North Carolina, South Carolina, Georgia, and Alabama. The Cherokee lived in villages. Each village had a large building that was the council house. When explorers from Europe first came to North America, the Cherokee Indians tried to be friendly to the newcomers. As the explorers began trying to take Cherokee lands, fighting began.

The Cherokee tried to sign peace treaties with the white men. They also tried living side by side with the settlers. After the Louisiana Purchase, the United States grew in size. Thomas Jefferson was the president. Many Cherokee Indians volunteered to move west and help settle the land there. Those Indians who stayed came together and formed the Cherokee Nation. Of course, not all people believed the Cherokee should have to move or give up their land. Many people argued for the rights of the Cherokee people, including respected men, such as Daniel Webster and Davy Crockett.

In 1828, gold was found on Cherokee land. People wanted the Cherokee removed from their land. The government of the United States agreed to remove the Indians. On May 28, 1830, President Andrew Jackson signed the Indian Removal Act. By 1838, all the Cherokee Indians were to give up their lands and move to an area in what is now Oklahoma. The government agreed to give the Cherokee people some money and supplies in return for their land. Many of the Cherokee people headed west. About 16,000 Cherokee did not leave. They stayed behind. Then on May 25, 1838, United States troops arrived to move the Cherokee. They forced them to leave their homes.

Not all the Cherokee took the same route. Most of the journey was done on foot. The trip took anywhere from three to six months. The Cherokee called it the trail where they cried. Sadly, about 4,000 people died on the Trail of Tears.

Name _____ **Date** _____

The following pages have questions based on the texts from Unit 23. You may look at the stories to help answer any questions. Use the back of the page if you need extra space for writing your answers.

1 How does Leeann feel about the work her mother is doing?

ⓐ angry

ⓑ proud

ⓒ frustrated

ⓓ embarrassed

2 Write the sentence from the text that helped you to answer #1.

_____

_____

_____

_____

3 What do the two texts have in common?

ⓐ Both are about the Trail of Tears.

ⓑ Both are about writing a book.

ⓒ Both are about a mother's love for her daughter.

ⓓ Both are about the early explorers from Europe.

4 What happened in 1828 that made people want Cherokee land?

ⓐ Floods ruined the other land.

ⓑ The Cherokee offered to give away some of the land.

ⓒ Gold was discovered on the land.

ⓓ Silver was found on some of the land.

5 Which president signed the Indian Removal Act?

ⓐ Andrew Jackson

ⓑ Franklin D. Roosevelt

ⓒ Andrew Johnson

ⓓ George Washington

6 Write two to three sentences to summarize the text "Signs of the Past."

_____

_____

_____

_____

_____

7 Write two facts you learned from the texts about the Cherokee Indians.

a. _____

_____

b. _____

_____

8 What is your opinion about the Cherokee Indians being removed from their land?

_____

_____

_____

_____

9 Explain the difference between a fact and an opinion.

A fact is _____.

An opinion is _____.

10 What does Leeann hope people will do after they read her mother's book?

(a) They will want to buy more copies of the book.

(b) They will pay more attention to the signs along the road.

(c) They will want to get her mother's autograph.

(d) They will learn about the Trail of Tears.

Time to Write!

Think about the Indian Removal Act and the Trail of Tears. Write facts about the events inside the rectangles. Then write your opinions about the events inside the circles.

Facts

Trail of Tears

Trail of Tears

Indian Removal Act

Indian Removal Act

Opinions

Trail of Tears

Indian Removal Act

The Fort

Angel ducked behind the colossal wall she had built using large boxes. She tried to be very quiet. She could not stay quiet. She giggled, and the minute she laughed, a large water balloon came crashing over her head. She had given away her location to her brother. The two boxes in front of her fell. Her brother had won, but they had a lot of fun hiding from each other and playing in her box fort.

Caleb came over and helped Angel set her boxes back on top of the other boxes. Things were a little wet where the water balloon had burst. The fort didn't look too bad. "Your wall of boxes did a good job of keeping you safe," Caleb said. "If you hadn't giggled, I wouldn't have known where you were."

"Your fort was good, too," Angel told her brother. "I liked how you built yours out of pillows. If you got tired, at least you had a place to take a nap," she joked.

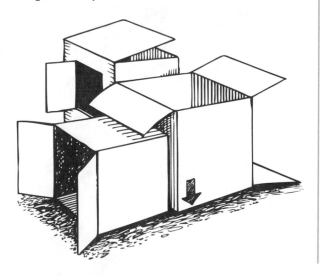

Angel and Caleb had been playing in their basement all day. Their mother had even told them it was okay to use water balloons inside the house as long as they cleaned up their mess when they were done. Their mother knew how much they wanted to play. It had been raining for four days. They both wanted to go outside and play, but it seemed like the rain was never going to stop. "Angel! Caleb!" Their mother's familiar voice came from upstairs. "Your cousins Logan and Gina are coming over to play today. Make sure you have something fun for everyone to do."

Angel looked at Caleb. She had a look that Caleb loved to see. It meant Angel had an exciting idea. "Let's build something new. We will put your pillows with my boxes. When Logan and Gina get here, we can build our own Great Wall like they have in China. We can use our wall to protect our land. Logan and Gina can help us find new things to build with, too. Then we will all be safe while we play on the other side of our Great Wall." Caleb liked the idea. He loved building things. He hoped they would get here soon. Maybe, he thought, rainy days weren't so bad after all.

The Great Wall of China

Throughout history, countries have tried to find ways to protect the people who live there. In ancient China, the people began building a wall to try to keep everyone safe from invaders. The wall was built in stages. It took years to complete. The first parts of the wall were built in 221 B.C. Soldiers, slaves, and poor people from the area were all sent to work on the wall.

Where is the wall? The Great Wall goes across the northern part of China. It is built in sections. The main part is more than 2,000 miles long! Roadways and steps were added to the top of the wall so soldiers could move more easily along the border of the wall. Being able to move along the wall helped the soldiers to defend the land.

Because the wall is so large, it was constantly being rebuilt and repaired. Some invaders were able to come through the gaps in the wall and enter China even though the wall was so big. Most of the rulers of China realized the wall was just too big and too expensive to take care of over the years.

Lookout towers were also built along the tower walls. These towers could be used to search for any enemies who might be coming. Soldiers also used the towers to signal other people along the wall and on the ground. They would use special signals to let others know if danger was nearby.

As trade began to grow between China and other nations, people from all over were amazed by the Great Wall. Most could not get over the size of the wall. Even though today many parts of the wall are gone or in ruins, the Great Wall of China is still something everyone should have the chance to see.

UNIT 24
QUESTIONS

Name

Date

The following pages have questions based on the texts from Unit 24. You may look at the stories to help answer any questions. Use the back of the page if you need extra space for writing your answers.

1 Why are Angel and Caleb playing inside?

    (a) It is dark outside.

    (b) Their mother won't let them go outside.

    (c) It is raining outside.

    (d) They don't want to play outside.

2 Define the word *rebuilt* as it is used in this sentence:

Because the wall is so large, it was constantly being rebuilt and repaired.

    (a) to tear down

    (b) to build again

    (c) to get help

    (d) to walk away

3 Explain why it was hard to take care of the wall.

_____

_____

_____

4 Why did people first build the Great Wall of China?

    (a) to keep people safe

    (b) to give everyone jobs

    (c) to get rid of extra bricks

    (d) to stop people from leaving

5 How does Caleb know where Angel is hiding?

    (a) She giggles.

    (b) She starts talking to Caleb.

    (c) She waves to her brother.

    (d) She stands up.

6 In your opinion, would a great wall help keep a country safe today? Explain your answer.

_____

_____

_____

_____

_____

7 Which paragraph in the text about the Great Wall best explains how large the wall is?

(a) paragraph 1

(b) paragraph 2

(c) paragraph 3

(d) paragraph 4

8 What type of relationship do you think Angel has with her brother, Caleb?

(a) They do not get along.

(b) They get along well with each other.

(c) They rarely talk to each other.

(d) They never play together.

9 Write two facts from the text about the Great Wall.

a. _____

_____

b. _____

_____

10 In the fiction text, who is coming over to play with Angel and Caleb?

_____

Time to Write!

The Great Wall of China has become something many people hope to get to see one day. Even when people see pictures of the wall, they know it is something special.

Imagine you have been asked to create a monument for your school. It does not have to be as large as the Great Wall, but it needs to be something that people will think is amazing. You can create anything except a wall.

Use the space below to draw and color your school's new monument. Then write a paragraph explaining what you will build and how it will be important to your school.

Name of the Monument: _____

_____

_____

_____

_____

_____

_____

_____

_____

The Northern Neighbor

Anna's mother slowed down the car as they got ready to cross the border into Canada. This was Anna's first time leaving the United States. She had her picture taken for her passport a few weeks earlier. Her mother had both their passports ready to show to the man at the border. He would tell them if it was okay for them to enter Canada.

The man smiled at Anna and her mother. He noticed how new her passport looked. He asked Anna if it was her first time leaving the country. She nodded yes. Then he reached over and put a special stamp on her passport. He told Anna to be sure to get lots of stamps on her passport. Each stamp would mean she had visited a new country. He told her she might have to ask each time to get her stamp but that someday she would like remembering all the places she'd seen. He told them both he hoped they would enjoy their stay in Canada.

Once they were in Canada, Anna couldn't stop looking out the window of the car. She wanted to see everything. It was all so new to her. Her mother had been reading a book to her about Canada once they knew they were making the trip. Anna knew that much of Canada was still a large wilderness. She also knew the temperatures were much colder than at her home in North Carolina. Anna hoped she would get to practice some of the French phrases her mother had taught her. She could not wait to say "good morning" and "hello" using her new French words.

As exciting as going to Canada was, Anna was even more excited about something else. Soon, they would get to see her grandparents. Anna's grandparents had moved to Canada three years ago. Her grandfather's business had moved his job from North Carolina to Canada. She used to see her grandparents almost every day. Now, she talked to them a lot on the phone, and she was able to see them when they talked thanks to the camera on her computer, but it just wasn't the same. Three years was too long to go without getting to wrap her arms around her grandparents. The car made a turn into a long driveway. Anna knew they were almost there. She already loved Canada.

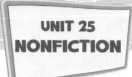
Canada is the northern neighbor to the United States. This large country shares the Rocky Mountains, the Great Lakes, and the St. Lawrence River with America. Alaska also shares a border with the country of Canada.

Many people recognize the Canadian flag when they see it. The flag's red maple leaf stands out from many other flag designs. The maple leaf is a national symbol of Canada.

Canada has a huge wilderness area, but the cities and towns are very modern. They have a good system of roads. In fact, they have one highway that is one of the longest in the world. It is so long that it goes across the country from the east coast to the west coast. It is 4,860 miles long! People who live in large cities use their cars to travel from place to place. Many also use the city buses to get where they need to be. People who live in Canada also use airplanes as well as trains to take them from place to place.

School in Canada is not very different from school in the United States. Children usually start school when they are about five years old. One big difference is that children in Canada learn to speak both English and French. This means that many Canadian citizens are bilingual, or can speak two languages.

When people think of sports in America, they often think of baseball. When people think of sports in Canada, they think of hockey. Hockey is the most popular sport in Canada. Canadians actually invented the game! Of course, Canadians also like many other sports. The official sport of Canada is lacrosse. Lacrosse is played with a long stick that has a net at the end of it. Players pass the ball to each other using the special stick.

The next time July 1 rolls around, think of Canada. This is the country's special holiday called Canada Day. It is much like Independence Day in the United States.

Name	Date

The following pages have questions based on the texts from Unit 25. You may look at the stories to help answer any questions. Use the back of the page if you need extra space for writing your answers.

1 Why are Anna and her mother going to Canada?

    (a) to see a new country

    (b) to have a reason to use Anna's new passport

    (c) to visit Anna's grandparents

    (d) to see Anna's father

2 What symbol is on Canada's flag?

    (a) a five pointed star

    (b) a maple leaf

    (c) an oak leaf

    (d) an eagle

3 Which paragraph from the text helped you to answer #2?

    (a) paragraph 1

    (b) paragraph 2

    (c) paragraph 3

    (d) The answer was not in any of the paragraphs.

4 Based on information from the text, many people in Canada are bilingual. What does the word *bilingual* mean?

    (a) They can speak two languages.

    (b) They are citizens in two different countries.

    (c) They speak French.

    (d) They have traveled to many countries.

5 What do the two texts have in common?

_____

_____

_____

6 Not including Alaska, the United States is Canada's _____ neighbor.

    (a) northern

    (b) western

    (c) southern

    (d) eastern

7 Which is a true statement about hockey?

    (a) Only Canadians play hockey.

    (b) Hockey is not popular in Canada.

    (c) Hockey is the official sport of Canada.

    (d) Hockey was invented in Canada.

8 What is Anna's opinion of Canada? Write a sentence from the text to support your answer.

_____

_____

_____

_____

9 What does a passport allow Anna to do?

    (a) cross the border into Canada

    (b) go to school in Canada

    (c) spend money in Canada

    (d) ride a train in Canada

10 Canada Day is similar to which holiday in America?

_____

Time to Write!

With your teacher's help, research a country you would NOT like to visit. Find out five facts about the country. Use the facts you found and the space below to write a report about a place you would never want to visit. Use the back of the page if you need more space to write.

Name of Country: _____

Fact 1: _____

_____

Fact 2: _____

_____

Fact 3: _____

_____

Fact 4: _____

_____

Fact 5: _____

_____

_____
_____
_____
_____
_____
_____
_____
_____

A Sad Truth

Tad sat across the lunch table from his best friend, Ben. Neither Tad nor Ben had much of an appetite today. Their teacher Mrs. Garrett had just read a book to them about World War II. Neither boy knew much about the war before Mrs. Garrett read the book. The book was about the heroes of World War II. The book was not about soldiers, but it was about everyday people who tried to save other people from harm and keep them safe. Tad had no idea so many people were in danger during the war. He knew a person must be very brave to be a soldier. He never knew how many other people also had to be brave.

"Tad," Ben began, "had you ever heard of the country Denmark before Mrs. Garrett read us that book?"

"No," Tad admitted, "but I looked it up on a map. It was right next to Germany. During World War II, being so close to Germany was not a good thing. Germany's ruler wanted to take over the world. He invaded Denmark. The king could do nothing to stop the soldiers who came in and took over his country."

Ben nodded his head. "It must have been hard on the king to know he should protect his people, but he couldn't."

Tad smiled a little. "But the book Mrs. Garrett read to us said that was what made the people of Denmark true heroes. They knew they couldn't fight the German soldiers and win, but they still found a way to fight. They helped hide the people the soldiers wanted to hurt. They helped save lives by getting many families to safe places."

Tad took the first bite of his sandwich. "It is good to know there are heroes in the real world and not just in comic books and movies."

Ben agreed with Tad. "It sure is, Tad. It sure is!"

Heroes of Denmark

World War II was a terrible war that involved countries all over the world. The United States joined the war in 1941. The war in Europe had been going on for much longer. One country in Europe that did not want to go to war was Denmark. Denmark is a small country that borders Germany. Since Germany started the war, Denmark was in a very bad location. Denmark's king did not want to go to war with Germany, but he wanted to protect his people. He tried hard to stay at peace with his German neighbors.

People who live in Denmark are called Danes. The Danish people knew the German soldiers wanted to take away some of the Jewish people who lived in Denmark. The people who lived in Denmark wanted to protect all of the citizens. They needed a plan to fight an army as large as Germany's. The people did not want any of their neighbors or friends to be hurt by the soldiers.

The Danish people heard about a German plan. The plan was not good for the Danes. German soldiers would be arriving in Denmark. The soldiers were planning to take away many of the Danish people from their homes and even from their country. The people knew they had to have a plan of their own. They decided to all work together and to hide anyone the German soldiers might want to take.

The people did not have a lot of time. They began hiding people wherever they could, so the German soldiers would not find them. They hid them anywhere they could find a place. The Danish people knew they could not keep everyone hidden for very long. The soldiers would be back. They would search better. They knew if they were going to keep everyone safe, they would have to get the people out of Denmark and to the country of Sweden. The people could be hidden on boats and taken to safety. Sweden was not involved in the war with Germany and wanted to help.

The fishermen worked with the Danes to rescue many people. In just a few days, over 7,000 people were taken to safety. The small country of Denmark made a huge difference to the world.

The following pages have questions based on the texts from Unit 26. You may look at the stories to help answer any questions. Use the back of the page if you need extra space for writing your answers.

1 Which country borders Denmark?

(a) Canada

(b) Japan

(c) Germany

(d) Mexico

2 Which word best describes how Tad feels after Mrs. Garrett read the book to the class?

(a) cheerful

(b) upset

(c) silly

(d) friendly

3 In your opinion, were the people of Denmark heroes? Why or why not?

_____

_____

_____

_____

4 Write two facts from the text "Heroes of Denmark."

a. _____

_____

b. _____

_____

5 Explain how you know your answers to #4 are facts and not opinions. They are facts

because _____

_____.

6 Explain the meaning of this sentence from the text "A Sad Truth":

"It is good to know there are heroes in the real world and not just in comic books and movies."

_____

_____

_____

7 Which country helped protect the people who were leaving Denmark?

(a) England

(b) France

(c) Germany

(d) Sweden

8 Write the sentence from the text that helped you to answer #7.

_____

_____

_____

_____

9 Who was after the people who lived in Denmark?

(a) the Germans

(b) the Americans

(c) the French

(d) the Italians

10 The people who were heroes during World War II are described as brave. Write your own definition for the word _brave_.

Brave means _____

_____

_____.

Time to Write!

Think about the people you know. Who do you know that is a real hero? Think about why you would call this person a hero. Think of as many reasons as you can to explain why this person is a hero to you.

Write about your special hero in the space below. Draw and color a picture of your hero in the empty box.

My hero is _____.

This person is my hero because . . .

_____

_____

_____

_____

_____

_____

_____

_____

_____

_____

_____

_____

_____

_____

_____

_____

_____

_____

Answer Key

Unit 1
1. b
2. The girls like to do things to help others in the community. They do volunteer work such as helping at the animal shelter. They do not expect to get paid for what they do. Much of what they mention in the text is helping others outside their families.
3. c
4. a
5. b
6. d
7. Answers will vary.
8. b
9. b
10. c

Unit 2
1. d
2. The use of "always" and "everyone" makes the statement an opinion.
3. Answers will vary.
4. a
5. Answers will vary.
6. b
7. Answers will vary.
8. c
9. d
10. Answers will vary.

Unit 3
1. b
2. b
3. d
4. She will check underneath her bed.
5. a
6. b
7.–8. Answers will vary.
9. b and c
10. d

Unit 4
1.–2. Answers will vary.
3. a
4. a
5. d
6. c
7. For many people, enjoying certain foods is all about what they see. (or)
   In other words, people judge their food by how it looks and not just by how it tastes.
8. d
9. b
10. b

Unit 5
1. They both have green eyes.
2. b
3. They both like studying traits that are passed down from one generation to the next.
4. b
5. d
6. a
7. He loved spending time with his great-grandmother.
8. Answers will vary.
9. c
10. Answers will vary.

Unit 6
1. b
2. c
3. Sadly, very few would find a way to get rich quick.
4. c
5. Answers will vary.
6. c
7. a
8.–9. Answers will vary.
10. She lives in an apartment in the city.

Unit 7
1. d
2. d
3. Answers will vary.
4. a
5. c
6. a. Stay inside.
   b. Check for weather warnings.
7. He will listen because he saw that his grandfather was right about the approaching storm.
8. b
9.–10. Answers will vary.

Unit 8
1. b
2. a
3. People from Japan brought it to America to celebrate the country's 100th birthday.
4. c
5. It is hard to kill and takes over everything around it.
6. b
7. Answers will vary.
8. b
9. because it was the perfect climate
10. Answers will vary.

Answer Key (cont.)

Unit 9
1. Answers will vary.
2. d
3. b
4. b
5.–6. Answers will vary.
7. c
8. b
9. a
10. Goods are items people need or can use.

Unit 10
1. c
2. a
3. a
4. Answers will vary.
5. a, b, and c
6. to help animals who are unable to live in their natural habitats
7. b
8. Both texts mention owls.
9. Answers will vary.
10. b

Unit 11
1. c
2. Answers will vary.
3. a
4. c
5. salt
6. a
7. He got salt water in his mouth from the ocean.
8. c
9. b
10. Answers will vary.

Unit 12
1. c
2. a
3. a
4. Answers will vary.
5. a
6.–8. Answers will vary.
9. c
10. Answers will vary.

Unit 13
1. a
2. c
3. Answers will vary.
4. to tell the main points
5. b
6. Answers will vary.
7. He will want to visit the zoo.

8. He knew the next time he visited his uncle, he would want to come here first.
9. hunting and loss of bamboo to eat
10. Answers will vary.

Unit 14
1. d
2. b
3. a
4. c
5. Answers will vary.
6. b
7.–8. Answers will vary.
9. a
10. Answers will vary.

Unit 15
1. a
2. c
3. keeps them safe and gives them shelter
4. b
5.–6. Answers will vary.
7. She is smiling at what she sees in the nest.
8. They use the creatures as food or transportation or in some other way.
9. **a**. bird
   b. raccoon or other forest animal like a raccoon
   c. turtle/tortoise
10. Answers will vary.

Unit 16
1. d
2. b
3. a
4. She had a sister who had a disability.
5. a
6. Answers will vary.
7. a
8. a
9. He was in a position of power to be able to help and get others to help.
10. holding/having

Unit 17
1. b
2. c
3. a
4. They are missing sugar cubes.
5. a
6.–7. Answers will vary.
8. b
9.–10. Answers will vary.

Answer Key (cont.)

Unit 18
1. b
2. The only thing she didn't like was the long drive to get to her father's house, but this year she was doing something new.
3. d
4. Answers may include the landing gear, the materials it was made from, etc.
5.–6. Answers will vary.
7. a
8. Answers will vary.
9. c
10. Answers will vary.

Unit 19
1. d
2. They both had something they wanted to overcome. (or) They both ran for president.
3. a
4. c
5. The virus caused Roosevelt to become paralyzed. (or) At the age of thirty-nine, Roosevelt could no longer walk unless someone was helping him.
6. Answers will vary.
7. b
8.–9. Answers will vary.
10. an immunization to keep people from becoming sick

Unit 20
1. The girls are going with their grandparents to see a dolphin show.
2. d
3. a
4. b
5. It helps the dolphin glide through the water.
6.–9. Answers will vary.
10. not in the wild

Unit 21
1. b
2. c
3. The electricity had been off for almost eight hours.
4. a
5. c
6.–7. Answers will vary.
8. One reason would be because there is not as much food in the winter.
9. c
10. She is taking care of the children. She is making hot chocolate, so they will stay warm.

Unit 22
1. d
2. c
3. b
4. a

5. to express their feelings or emotions
6. b
7. if they are sad
8. a
9. He is too happy.
10. Answers will vary.

Unit 23
1. b
2. Now she was also very proud of her mother.
3. a
4. c
5. a
6.–8. Answers will vary.
9. A fact can be proven to be true. An opinion is simply what someone believes to be true or how someone feels about something.
10. d

Unit 24
1. c
2. b
3. It was too large.
4. a
5. a
6. Answers will vary.
7. b
8. b
9. Answers will vary.
10. their cousins, Logan and Gina

Unit 25
1. c
2. b
3. b
4. a
5. Canada
6. c
7. d
8. Anna loves Canada. "She already loved Canada."
9. a
10. Independence Day (July 4)

Unit 26
1. c
2. b
3.–4. Answers will vary.
5. . . . they can be proven to be true.
6. Answers will vary.
7. d
8. Sweden was not involved in the war with Germany and wanted to help.
9. a
10. showing courage

Meeting Standards

Each passage and activity meets one or more of the following Common Core State Standards © Copyright 2010. National Governors Association Center for Best Practices and Council of Chief State School Officers. All rights reserved. For more information about the Common Core State Standards, go to *http://www.corestandards.org/* or *http://www.teachercreated.com/standards/*.

Reading: Literature	Passages and Activities
Key Ideas and Details	
ELA.RL.4.1: Refer to details and examples in a text when explaining what the text says explicitly and when drawing inferences from the text.	all fiction
ELA.RL.4.3: Describe in depth a character, setting, or event in a story or drama, drawing on specific details in the text (e.g., a character's thoughts, words, or actions).	all fiction
Craft and Structure	
ELA.RL.4.4: Determine the meaning of words and phrases as they are used in a text, including those that allude to significant characters found in mythology (e.g., Herculean).	all fiction
Range of Reading and Level of Text Complexity	
ELA.RL.4.10: By the end of the year, read and comprehend literature, including stories, dramas, and poetry, in the grades 4–5 text complexity band proficiently, with scaffolding as needed at the high end of the range.	all fiction
Reading: Informational Text	**Passages and Activities**
Key Ideas and Details	
ELA.RI.4.1: Refer to details and examples in a text when explaining what the text says explicitly and when drawing inferences from the text.	all nonfiction
ELA.RI.4.2: Determine the main idea of a text and explain how it is supported by key details; summarize the text.	Unit 13, Unit 15
Craft and Structure	
ELA.RI.4.5: Describe the overall structure (e.g., chronology, comparison, cause/effect, problem/solution) of events, ideas, concepts, or information in a text or part of a text.	all nonfiction

Integration of Knowledge and Ideas	
ELA.RI.4.9: Integrate information from two texts on the same topic in order to write or speak about the subject knowledgeably.	all nonfiction
Range of Reading and Level of Text Complexity	
ELA.RI.4.10: By the end of year, read and comprehend informational texts, including history/social studies, science, and technical texts, in the grades 4–5 text complexity band proficiently, with scaffolding as needed at the high end of the range.	all nonfiction
Writing	**Passages and Activities**
Text Types and Purposes	
ELA.W.4.1: Write opinion pieces on topics or texts, supporting a point of view with reasons and information.	Unit 10, Unit 11, Unit 15, Unit 26
ELA.W.4.2: Write informative/explanatory texts to examine a topic and convey ideas and information clearly.	Unit 2, Unit 5, Unit 14, Unit 23, Unit 24
ELA.W.4.3: Write narratives to develop real or imagined experiences or events using effective technique, descriptive details, and clear event sequences.	Unit 4, Unit 7, Unit 8, Unit 12, Unit 18, Unit 19, Unit 20, Unit 21
Production and Distribution of Writing	
ELA.W.4.4: Produce clear and coherent writing in which the development and organization are appropriate to task, purpose, and audience.	Unit 1, Unit 6, Unit 17, Unit 22
Research to Build and Present Knowledge	
ELA.W.4.7: Conduct short research projects that build knowledge through investigation of different aspects of a topic.	Unit 9, Unit 13, Unit 16, Unit 25
Range of Writing	
ELA.W.4.10: Write routinely over extended time frames (time for research, reflection, and revision) and shorter time frames (a single sitting or a day or two) for a range of discipline-specific tasks, purposes, and audiences.	all nonfiction and fiction